John Keble
Saint of Anglicanism

John R. Griffin

John Keble
Saint of Anglicanism

 MERCER
UNIVERSITY PRESS

ISBN 0-86554-249-X

The paper used in this publication meets
the minimum requirements of American National Standard
for Information Sciences—Permanence of Paper
for Printed Library Materials, ANSI Z39.48-1984.

Library of Congress Cataloging-in-Publication Data
Griffin, John R.
John Keble, saint of Anglicanism.
Bibliography: p. 119
Includes index.
1. Keble, John, 1792-1866. 2. Church of England—
Clergy—Biography. 3. Anglican Communion—England—
Clergy—Biography. 4. Oxford movement—England—
History. 5. England—Church history 19th century.
I. Title.
BX5199.K3G75 1987 283'.3[B] 86-31210
ISBN 0-86554-249-X (alk. paper)

Contents

Acknowledgments

In doing my research for this book, I have incurred numerous debts to the library staffs of many universities and colleges in this country and Great Britain. I wish to acknowledge a special debt of gratitude to the library staffs of the Bodleian Library, the British Museum, Keble College, Pusey House, Birmingham Oratory of St. Philip, Lambeth Palace Library, Liddon House, and the Public Records Office. In this country, I have been a frequent guest at Nashotah House, Wisconsin, and I have always been generously received. Also, I wish to thank the library staffs of Princeton, Yale, and Northwestern universities. I want to thank my colleagues on the library staff at the University of Southern Colorado, especially Mrs. Beverly Moore, Miss Kristine Sternjholm, and Mr. Daniel Sullivan.

I also thank the Faculty Research Committee of the University of Southern Colorado and the American Philosophical Society for several grants that enabled me to travel to the various places named above. Without their help, this work could not have been done.

On a personal level, I wish to express my indebtedness to several colleagues and administrators at my university for the practical and philosophical support they have given to my research: Mr. Ronald Whitsitt, Dr. James Kashner, Dr. Robert Shirley, and Dr. James Sublette. I have been very well served by Mrs. Micki Markowski, who typed the manuscript through its various stages, and Mr. and Mrs. William McDonald who proofread the work in its early phases.

Most of all, I want to thank my wife in the most extravagant terms that her modesty and intelligence will allow. She has given this and other projects all the support that was needed, but my debt to her is even greater. From her example and precept I have come to appreciate even more the achievement of John Keble. *The Christian Year* is not only great poetry—it is true.

Introduction

Shortly after his conversion, John Henry Newman was asked to write a review essay on a new book of poetry by his friend and mentor, John Keble. The book's title, *Lyra Innocentium,* suggests its subject matter—songs about children. Newman praised the poetry and especially its author, for Keble had refused to join in Anglican attacks on those who had recently gone over to Rome. If Keble had referred to the converts as "doubting Thomases" or children who had failed in obedience to "their elders," that was at least more charitable than the slanders that had been published in the Anglo-Catholic press since Newman's conversion in November 1845.

Keble's silence about other English church matters was more difficult to explain. Twenty years earlier, in his first volume of poetry—*The Christian Year*—he sounded the call for a reform of the Church of England. His call for reform inspired the Oxford Movement that eventually led to Newman's conversion. Newman wondered how Keble could be silent on problems in his church since these problems were more obvious in 1845 than they were when *The Christian Year* was first published: "Is it that singing-birds are silent when a storm is at hand, and that the evil in his church is too awful and imminent for verse?"[1]

Anglican scholars have always bristled at Newman's suggestion that there was anything Roman in the teachings of John Keble. His teachings and doctrines were learned from his clerical father, John Keble, Sr., whose religious traditions went back to the Caroline divines of the seventeenth century. Those traditions had become "less and less prominent"[2] in the early nineteenth century, but there were never any new assertions in the doctrines of either man. As John Keble's most recent biographer has written,

> . . . when Newman and Froude were all enthusiasm for some item of Catholic faith or practice, which had burst upon them with the force of a new revelation, Keble would nod approval and remark in tones of highest commendation, "Yes, that is exactly what my father taught me."[3]

It was Keble's background in the tradition of "northern" Catholicism that saved him for the English church. If Newman had been raised in that tradition, there would have been no need for him to go over to Rome.

Keble's heritage of English Catholic doctrines enabled him to act with Christian charity towards Newman and the others who did go over in 1845 or later. As the most learned member of the founders of the first Oxford Movement, he viewed the Catholic claims of the English church as unaffected by the mounting protests of his coreligionists. Indeed, he interpreted Newman's conversion as a gesture destined to bring the Church of England and the Church of Rome closer together. It was Keble, by reason of his learning and holiness, who introduced the note of friendly neu-

---

[1]John Henry Newman, "John Keble," *Dublin Review* 20 (June 1846): 434-61; reprinted in *Essays, Critical and Critical* (London: Longman's, Green, & Co., 1878) 452.

[2]Clifton Kelway, *The Story of the Catholic Revival* (London: Philip Allan, 1933) 1.

[3]Georgina Battiscombe, *John Keble: A Study in Limitations* (New York: Alfred A. Knopf, 1964) 11.

trality and openness towards Rome that characterized the second (post-1845) Oxford Movement.[4]

I

In this study I will propose a new version of Keble's life and achievement; and while I agree with the Anglican idea that Keble was and is the "saint of Anglicanism," I will argue that the key to his sanctity is very different from what has been routinely assumed by most of his biographers, and by historians of the Oxford Movement.

The next chapter is a fairly extensive revision of the accepted version of Keble's early life and training. From that revision I propose a new reading of *The Christian Year* and his other literary works, as well as a fresh examination of his much disputed role in the first and second Oxford Movements. A great difficulty in studying Keble is that while he is praised by almost everyone who has written about the Victorian church, he is seldom read. He has always been regarded as too simple in his life and teachings to warrant any close examination of what he wrote or taught in his lifetime. In review of a study on Keble's poetry, E. R. Norman has written, "Keble's importance is as a saint, not as a poet or critic. He inspired others because they saw in his simplicity a luminous presence removed from the normal expectations of human personality."[5] The best that can now be said of his poetry is that it is fairly good religious poetry—the worst, that it is "a pint-pot of simple measures."[6]

Keble's other claim upon a modern's attention has also been challenged. In the *Apologia* Newman described Keble as the "true and primary author" of the Oxford Movement and his sermon

---

[4]Cf. Arthur Allchin, "The Via Media—An Anglican Reevaluation," in *Newman: A Portrait Restored,* ed. John Coulson (London: Sheed and Ward, 1965) 68-70.

[5]Edward Norman, "John Keble," *Times Literary Supplement,* 25 February 1977, 211.

[6]Ian Jack, *English Literature, 1815-1832* (Oxford: Clarendon Press, 1963) 149.

"National Apostasy" as its beginning.[7] But the Newman tribute to Keble has been dismissed as "myth."[8] Keble was too much of a saint—too simple in his life and aspirations—to have begun the movement. Rather, he served as the "moral" guardian to his younger and more aggressive friends (Newman and Pusey); and when he accepted a living at Hursley in 1835, he furnished the "pastoral" model for the Tractarians.[9]

I will suggest that there are good reasons to follow Newman's judgment on Keble's primary place in the first Oxford Movement, and to accept Newman's praise of *The Christian Year* as a "classic in our language." As a writer, and especially as an apologist for the Catholic principle of Anglicanism, Keble is far more complex than has been assumed. Those who have described Keble as a pious but ineffective imitator of Wordsworth's *Lyrical Ballads* will note that in doing the research of this study, I have uncovered an early essay by Keble about his alleged mentor. The essay is strong in its criticism of several of the central themes in Wordsworth's poetry and criticism, and it published at a time when Keble was composing *The Christian Year*. There are two other "new" essays by Keble, and each reflects an aspect of Keble's thought that has not been acknowledged by scholars.

The final revision in this study is in my examination of Keble's alleged ecumenism of 1845 and later. As in the above, evidence that Keble did not regard the differences that separated the two churches as "minor" can be found in what he actually wrote and said in the critical years just before and after Newman's conversion. During this time Keble published a series of pamphlets and sermons on the "Roman" question. Each expresses strong criticism of the converts and the new religion that they accepted. In this material we also find an interesting apologetic for himself and other Anglicans who shared his attitudes or principles.

---

[7] Wilfred Ward, ed., *Apologia Pro Vita Sua* (London: Everyman Books, 1912) 42.

[8] Frank Cross, *Newman* (London: Philip Allan, 1933) 162.

[9] Owen Chadwick, ed., *The Mind of the Movement* (Stanford CA: Stanford University Press, 1960) 19.

Through an examination of this material, his poetry, pamphlets, and sermons, I will argue that Keble was more creative in his apologetics than has been assumed.

Biographers tend to exaggerate almost every saint's life. No miracles have ever been ascribed to Keble's influence, but the idea that his teachings reflected what he had learned from his father is, in part, an invention.

Since I am suggesting an alternative commentary on his life, it might be useful to explain the origins of what might be called the Keble legend. In the *Apologia* Newman describes one of Keble's most characteristic mannerisms when he remarks that Keble was always "happier, when he could speak or act under some such primary or external sanction."[10] The reading of this passage has been that the teachings of 1833 were a reflection of his father's ideals since his father, by all accounts, was a "primary sanction." Newman means, however, that it was almost impossible to find out what Keble thought on most subjects: "You did not know where to find him."[11]

Another source for the current version of Keble's background is John Taylor Coleridge's *Memoir of the Rev. John Keble,* published two years after Keble's death in 1866. Coleridge had known Keble for more than fifty years, and a major theme in the *Memoir* is the strict sense of obedience that Keble observed towards his father. The elder Keble was an old-fashioned "high-churchman," according to Coleridge, and from such a description it might be inferred that the ideology of 1833 was a reflection of that kind of churchmanship.[12] Yet Coleridge does not use the word *Catholic* to describe Keble's "principles" of religion or those of his father, and since he quickly passes over the Tractarian phase of Keble's life, it can be argued that the Oxford Movement was an interrup-

---

[10]*Apologia Pro Vita Sua* (14th ed.; London: Longman's, Green, & Co., 1900) 290.

[11]Charles S. Dessain and Thomas Gornall, eds., *Letters and Diaries of John Henry Newman,* vol. 26 (Oxford: Clarendon Press, 1974) 375.

[12]John T. Coleridge, *Memoir of the Rev. John Keble* (Oxford: James Parker, 1868) 7.

tion of his normal course of thought. Newman supplies more information about the extent of Keble's role in the Oxford Movement when he notes that at the time of "National Apostasy," Keble was under the influence of someone other than his father—Hurrell Froude, a professed radical in 1833.

The radical ideal in Keble's sermon and the first volume of the *Tracts for the Times* was a break from the traditions Keble inherited from his father, and in that brief "parenthesis"[13] (Keble's word for his part in the Oxford Movement) we can see why Keble's position after 1845 was so militantly anti-Roman. After his brief flirtation with the idea of a complete separation of church and state, an impoverished clergy, and an apostolic episcopate, Keble retreated into a more common form of churchmanship. This interpretation of Tractarian ideology will be developed in a later chapter, but Keble's retreat from the principles of 1833 suggests that Keble sometimes changed his mind, even on vital issues.

If I have not accepted the standard version of Keble's holiness, the present work ultimately does enhance the notion that Keble was a saint, and perhaps higher on the spiritual ladder than even his most devoted biographers have realized. When Newman describes the English church as a "half-way house" between Rome and atheism, he invokes a rigorous logic that few could follow. Keble rested in that house and did his best to assist others in resting in the church where "God had placed them"; but it is a grotesque oversimplification to suggest that he had a complete or perfect confidence in his place in that church. Keble lived very much in the presence of religious doubt, and his ability to work through that doubt in defending himself and others of a kindred mind is one of the great feats of Anglican apologetics in the Victorian era. This study examines the variations and development of that apologetic.

---

[13]Isaac Williams, *Autobiography,* ed. George Prevost (London: Longman's, Green, & Co., 1892) 113.

Chapter I

A Brief Life

Keble's Father

Keble's father was the vicar of St. Aldwyn's church in Coln, a region in the southeastern part of England. He lived in his own house in Fairford, three miles from the church, a circumstance that raises the suspicion that he may have been "irregular" in the performance of his duties.

The only evidence about the religious views and practices of Keble's father is admittedly weak. On permanent loan at Lambeth Palace Library is a collection of his sermons, with the dates of delivery on the back of each.[1] The careful dating of the sermons suggests that the collection is complete and that he never wrote more than ten sermons in his life. Each was given many times in the course of his long ministry at St. Aldwyn's, and numerous Sundays and feast days were missed.

The religious views in the sermons are not easily described. There is no mention of the word Christ, nor is there any commentary on scriptural events. Christianity—"Xtianity" as he wrote

---

[1]John Keble, Sr., "Sermons," in Williams Manuscript Collection, Box 3, Lambeth Palace Library, London.

it—is a social force in the life of man, not a collection of doctrines or creeds. There is traditional Protestantism in his assertion that the Bible is a complete guide to the Christian life, not a "tardy + partial revelation" to be complemented by tradition or the church (the Catholic view). There are vigorous attacks, moreover on any Eucharistic doctrine that might suggest "Transubstantiation + a whole train of absurdities too ridiculous to be named," as well as attacks on doctrines that Keble took up late in his life, especially the doctrine of Purgatory. As might be expected from the doctrines that Keble's father ridiculed, it is not surprising to find no mention of the word *Catholic* or any of the later Tractarian doctrines.

The attitude expressed toward the Methodists and Catholics, however, was based only in part on the doctrinal errors of both groups. His basic animus against both was rather that each posed a threat to the social order, especially the alliance of church and state. The father was in all likelihood not a high-churchman, except in his pronounced Toryism and keen dislike of all non-Anglican religions. From a doctrinal point of view, he seems to have been, like most of his contemporaries, a liberal churchman in his apparent contempt for even the idea of doctrine.

There may be materials that would alter the above ideas about the religious milieu of his son, but it might be remembered that one of the major themes in *The Christian Year* is a call for reform among lower clergy, an idea that Keble might have learned from the example of his father. But if the father was not zealous in his life as a clergyman, he proved to be an excellent tutor to his two sons (John and Tom). With a superb piece of unconscious irony, Keble's biographer has urged that the father was a good clergyman *because* he gave personal tuition to his two sons.[2]

Very little else is known about the man. He was a graduate of Corpus Christi College, and maintained friendly relations with officials of the college and nourished the ideal of sending his sons to his old college. His ability to tutor his sons in Latin and Greek

---

[2]Georgina Battiscombe, *John Keble: A Study in Limitations* (New York: Alfred A. Knopf, 1964) 8ff.

suggests an enduring concern for lessons that he had learned at Oxford; and the abiding interest of John Keble in certain Anglican church fathers, notably Hooker and Leslie, may have been learned from the senior clergyman.

The domestic life of the Keble family was very happy. John Keble maintained a good relationship with all of his brothers and sisters throughout his life—unlike Pusey or Newman, whose households were very early beset with internal strife. It might only be added that the region in which Keble grew up and later selected for his residence was exceptionally beautiful, very like that area celebrated in Gilbert White's *Natural History of Selbourne.* Scholars who have praised both men for the sanctity of their lives in taking up such abodes may never have seen Hursley or Coln. For certain kinds of temperament, the countryside is at least as rewarding as life at Oxford or in some episcopal see.

The most conspicuous result of Keble's upbringing was a love of nature in its external form (a love that was later transformed into the poetry of *The Christian Year*) and an abiding respect for his father. As Coleridge observed, Keble never made a move without consulting his father.[3] Still, the idea that Keble taught what he had learned from his father is without scholarly evidence. The only mention of his father's teaching comes in a letter written less than a year before the Oxford Movement, a letter in which Keble vigorously censured the Eucharistic views of a friend (A. Perceval) for their tendency to "turn good young Protestants into Papists." In that letter, as well as in all earlier correspondence, Keble habitually referred to the Church of England as Protestant, and he defended those who had turned "protestant in the sixteenth century." At the end of that letter, he invoked the English Reformers as the only guide to religious doctrine. He concluded with the remark that he was writing in the presence of his father.[4]

---

[3]John T. Coleridge, *Memoir of the Rev. John Keble,* (Oxford: James Parker,1868) 7.

[4]John Keble to Arthur Perceval, June 1832, in Keble-Perceval Correspondence, Pusey House, Oxford.

Keble's Life to 1833

There are few records about John Keble's earliest years. He was born in 1792, the second of five children. His companions, until he went to Oxford, were probably his brothers and sisters for, as a tentative member of upper classes, he would not have been allowed to play with children of the local farmers.

At the age of fourteen he entered Corpus Christi, graduating four years later with highest honors in Classics and Mathematics, a feat that had not been accomplished since the Double First of Sir Robert Peel a few years earlier. The letters from college reveal a pleasant existence there, with wine parties, breakfasts with friends, and a growing friendship with Thomas Arnold and John Taylor Coleridge. Both friends later achieved brilliant success based partly on great personal endowments and, as both men avowed, partly on the competitive spirit that was a part of college life.[5] Keble entered into those competitions as freely as the father of "muscular Christianity" (Dr. Arnold) and John T. Coleridge, a later spokesman for the Protestant Church of England against Catholics in Victorian England. Keble probably imbibed some of the same spirit while at Corpus Christi, and we can tell something about Keble's religious outlook in noting that his friends were professed Protestants of a non-Evangelical type, for the Evangelicals regarded competition as one of the deadly sins.[6]

In the area of academic competition, few of that generation even came close to Keble; still, it is ironic that he failed to win any of the annual prizes for poetry. After graduation, Keble achieved another honor—the highest that Oxford could then confer—an Oriel Fellowship, which as a contemporary reported, "invested him with a bright halo and something of awe in the eyes of an undergraduate."[7] There were no formal duties at Oriel, and Keble returned to assist his father after a year's residence at Oriel.

---

[5]Arthur Stanley, ed., *Life and Letters of Dr. Thomas Arnold,* 2 vols. (London: B. Fellowes, 1844) 1:14-32.

[6]Reginald Wilberforce, *Life of Samuel Wilberforce,* 3 vols. (London: John Murray, 1880) 1:19.

[7]Thomas Mozley, *Reminiscences Chiefly of Oriel College and the Oxford Movement,* 2 vols. (Boston: Houghton Mifflin Co., 1882) 1:37.

Keble returned to Oriel two years later with (apparently) feelings of guilt for giving up his clerical duties. He justified the act by noting that his role as Fellow was pastoral in character. His comments may have been a rationalization, but Keble really did believe that teaching at every level was a moral act. There were obvious advantages in being at Oriel. It was an easy life, and a fellowship was often a stepping-stone to something higher. In Keble's case, he met Sir William Heathcote, who later gave him his living at Hursley.

Oriel was recognized as the best college at Oxford at that time. The Fellows were a group of brilliant men, including several who would later become famous for their religious liberalism and Protestantism (including Richard Whately and Renn Hampden) and their heated opposition to the ideas of the Oxford Movement. One of Keble's biographers has suggested that Keble was probably uncomfortable in that "Noetic" (for its emphasis on intellectual excellent and speculative inquiry) atmosphere and that Keble, had he been less fortified in the high-church tradition, might have abandoned some of his earlier principles.

> It was to be expected that he would be profoundly influenced by his daily, almost hourly, contact with some of the most distinguished personages, the most vigorous minds and the most attractive characters at Oxford. He would be moulded into the prevalent Noetic shape, his dialectical and philosophical powers developed, his High-Church notions if not abandoned, at least reconsidered.[8]

The truth is that Keble was not a high-churchman at this time and that he got on handsomely with all whom he met at Oriel. Whately commented on his early affection for Keble,[9] and it has been noted that Keble and Hampden were close friends at that time.[10] One of Keble's pupils from this period (Lord Vane) noted with astonishment Keble's later participation in the Tractarian

---

[8]Battiscombe, *John Keble,* 29.

[9]Elizabeth Whately, ed., *Life and Correspondence of Richard Whately,* 2 vols. (London: Longman's, Green, & Co., 1866) 1:38.

[10]Stanley, *Life and Letters of Dr. Thomas Arnold,* 1:74.

opposition to Hampden's liberalism.[11] What I believe can be drawn from the evidence of Keble's friends is that he was as liberal as any of the others at Oriel.

From this collection of persons I think it is reasonable to suggest that Keble's "principles" of religion were rather like those of his friends. The few brief comments on religious issues in his many letters to Coleridge from this period reflect several of the ideas in his father's sermons, notably that the Bible was the exclusive source of religious truth and that if a principle or duty could be found in scripture, it was binding on the individual; otherwise, the individual Christian was allowed an enormous freedom of choice in what he was obliged to accept. Once Keble told Coleridge that if he found Calvinism in scripture, he would be a Calvinist.[12]

There is one other feature in Keble's life during his time as a Fellow of Oriel. No one has ever been able to determine how individuals were selected for that great honor, but almost certainly it was not grades alone that prompted nomination. Mark Pattison remarks that persons were selected for their originality or promise of originality, a trait that Keble must have shared with some of his Noetic peers.[13]

A new set of friends entered Keble's life during his later years at Oriel: Richard Hurrell Froude, Robert and Henry Wilberforce, and Isaac Williams. Each of these persons paid tribute to the moral influence that Keble exercised over their lives, but there was relatively no discussion of his, or their own, views on matters of doctrine except that each became more serious about religious life.[14]

The final friend that might be mentioned at this stage of Keble's life is Newman, who, after failure in his pursuit of academic honors,

---

[11]*Letters and Diaries of John Henry Newman,* ed. Charles Dessain and Thomas Gornall (Oxford: Clarendon Press, 1974) 26:375.

[12]John Keble to John Coleridge, 29 March 1817, in Keble-Coleridge Correspondence, 3 vols., Bodleian Library, Oxford; hereafter CC.

[13]Mark Pattison, *Memoirs* (London: Macmillan Co., 1882) 131.

[14]Cf. Piers Brendon, *Richard Hurrell Froude and the Oxford Movement* (London: Paul Elek, 1974) passim.

was elected a Fellow of Oriel in 1822. Newman confessed to his mother that he cringed at the prospect of calling Keble, "the first man in Oxford," by his last name, but he was instantly charmed by complete lack of affection in Keble's manner.[15] The Keble correspondence with Newman at this stage had none of the intimacy of the later years, and it may have been Newman's religious outlook that created the barrier—Newman was still an evangelical and already deeply intent on an arduous Christian life.

The next year Keble left to take his first living at Southrop, a region near his father. In 1827 the Provostship of Oriel was open to election. Keble was regarded as a leading candidate for the position. He was nominated by Froude as the very best man for the job, but Pusey and Newman supported a rival candidate (Hawkins) believing that Keble was too unworldly for the task. "We are not electing an angel, but a Provost," said Newman by way of explanation. Thinking that Keble was not really interested in the job, Newman was quite candid in his opposition and received a gentle rebuff from Keble that caused him to think that Keble actually did want to become Provost.[16] The relevant item is that Keble's clerical vocation was not completely settled at the time, though he was then past thirty.

There are two other events of major importance at this stage of Keble's life: the publication of *The Christian Year* and the Oxford Professorship of Poetry. Keble had planned to keep revising his poetry. But friends encouraged him to get the work completed and in print as a means "of doing good." The remarks of Thomas Arnold are a fair measure of the early response to the poems.

> I do not know whether you have ever seen John Keble's Hymns. . . . I live in hope that he will be induced to publish them; and it is my firm opinion that nothing equal to them exists in our language: the wonderful knowledge of Scripture, the purity of heart, and the richness of the poetry which they exhibit, I never saw

---

[15]Dessain and Gornell, *Letters and Diaries*, 1:131.

[16]Ibid., 30:107-108.

paralleled. If they are not published, it will be a great neglect of doing good.[17]

Whately was also excited about the poems and equally emphatic in urging that they be published. However, the decision to have them published probably came from Keble's desire to please his father. The poems were an instant success at Oxford, and one of Keble's friends noted that most of the Fellows and undergraduates quickly learned them by heart.[18]

Also important to Keble's growing reputation was the Professorship of Poetry, an appointment of five years duration (Keble was elected for a second five years) with four lectures a year. The lectures were given in Latin, a tradition not broken until 1857 when Matthew Arnold, Keble's godson, gave them in English.

At the time of these achievements, Keble was assisting his father at Fairford and had been vicar in several other places. There are almost no comments about religious questions in the correspondence, but Thomas Arnold's words on Keble's assistance in resolving his (Arnold's) personal problems are interesting for several reasons. First, Arnold and Keble were very close friends, as suggested by Arnold's request that Keble be godfather to his first born (Matthew). This friendship has been glossed over by Keble's biographers, but it existed for a longer time than any of his later friendships. The second point is that Keble, contrary to the assertions of some of his biographers, was very helpful in the problem of resolving religious doubt. On this latter point, Arnold wrote to the Coleridges,

> He [Keble] advised me to drop the study of the controversy, and to work actively at my daily Duties, and to study the Scriptures practically as he considered my doubts to be a disease of Mind, owing to its want of Submission + Humility. But my only Difficulty is this: how ought I, on Protestant Principles to silence my doubts—by the Authority of the Church, itself confessedly fail-

---

[17]Thomas Arnold to John Coleridge, July 1825, in Letters of Thomas Arnold, 1817-1842, CC.

[18]Mozley, *Reminiscences*, 1:219.

lible [*sic*]. . . . I am afraid of being prejudiced by worldly Motives. But I have practically followed K's advice.[19]

The letter is vital to our understanding of Keble's method in handling religious difficulties. Arnold and, I suspect, Keble regarded the Church of England as Protestant at this time. Scripture, according to Keble, was to be studied for its practical application, rather than for any doctrinal content. One cannot say how often the "Roman" question was raised in Keble's circle of friends, but his response that doubt was the result of pride and should be regarded as a kind of mental illness is one of the themes of Keble's life, before and after the Oxford Movement. Arnold's other brief comment on the subject of "worldly Motives" reminds us that membership in the English church was essential for any kind of material prosperity in a religious life and should be remembered by those who fault Newman and the others for going to Rome. The most interesting feature of Arnold's letter, however, is in the implicit contradiction that it poses to Keble's many biographers, who have suggested that he was so very secure in his own faith that he could never understand the problems that others might have with matters of religion.

There are other letters from this period that tell us something about Keble's early religious development and his life as a rural vicar. Shortly after he left Oriel he was approached by his friend John Coleridge, editor of the literature section of the *Quarterly Review,* to write for the journal—then the most prestigious conservative publication of the time. Keble contributed several essays, including a review essay on the subject of preaching. Keble agreed with the author, whose book he was reviewing, that the basic ideal of all preaching was to draw attention to the subject of the sermon, rather than to the speaker. After three years as an infrequent contributor, Keble gave up what might have been a profitable venture with the *Quarterly,* for he was angered at the religious tone of the review, and in particular at its attacks on the English Socinians. He explained his attitude to Coleridge:

---

[19]Thomas Arnold to John Coleridge, 18 February 1817, Arnold Letters, CC.

". . . to tell you the truth, we are not quite satisfied with Rennell [the friend] at Oxford, he is too violent in his orthodoxy even for us."[20]

His specific complaint was the quarrel between the Bishop of London and some Unitarians in his diocese, a controversy that led to an anti-Unitarian essay in the *Quarterly*. Before the essay appeared, Keble complained about Rennell's "itch to attack the Socinians," and when it was published he gave up his professional relationship with the journal.

> I wrote to Rennell by tomorrow's post, in order to decline doing Gibbon . . . partly because I do not at all like the Spirit + stile of it on certain subjects. In the last number for instance the virulence of abuse against the Socinians.[21]

Such a defense, however tacit, of the Unitarians against an Anglican bishop suggests that Keble's early religious views were more liberal, perhaps, than those of even his father.

The first sign of high-churchmanship came ten years later when Keble witnessed some of the labor riots at Durham. His introduction, however, to that kind of churchmanship was political, rather than religious, in inspiration. At the time, Keble laughed at some of the bishops, and his growing friendship with Froude and Newman seems to have had no immediate effect on his anti-doctrinal position.

Yet in the midst of all the various documents that support the idea that Keble was a Tory Protestant churchman until he was nearly forty, there is one curiosity. In an essay of 1846 Newman remarked,

> . . . those who knew Oxford twenty or thirty years ago, say that, while other college rooms were ornamented with pictures of Napoleon on horseback . . . there was one man, a young and rising one, in whose rooms . . . might be seen the Madonna di Sistro.[22]

---

[20]Keble to Coleridge, 10 April 1815, CC.

[21]Ibid., 24 January 1816, CC.

[22]"John Keble," in *Essays, Critical and Historical,* (London: Longman's Green, & Co., 1878) 2:452.

The picture of the Madonna must have been unusual for that age. Even within the invariably narrow circle of Keble's later high-church friends there was strong opposition to the idea that there was anything distinctive about Mary. The picture and the poems about Mary in *The Christian Year* suggest a personal cult that Keble may have practiced through his last forty years. The picture illustrates a severe independence in religious principles that we do not normally associate with John Keble.

At the time the first volume of poems was published, Keble was by and large a liberal Protestant who supported the Reformation and disliked Rome. This ancestral Protestantism explains why so "little of the peculiar Tractarian teaching appears in the book."[23] The poems, apart from the idea of reforming the spiritual life of the English church, do not belong to the Tractarian movement.

Keble as Priest

Keble once remarked that the biographies of poets were generally unsatisfactory because it was impossible to describe the life of one who was ultimately a mystery. How much greater, then, is the problem of describing the life of a country parson. That he seldom discussed his ministry or his own spiritual interests in any detail is ambiguous. It might mean that neither subject interested him, but it is more likely that he would never have made any religious professions that sounded like egotism.

The exception to this general silence on spiritual matters are the letters that Keble sent just before his ordination. Unlike many of his fellow clergy, Keble did approach his ordination with great soul-searching on the question of his personal worthiness, and he asked Coleridge to tell him of any faults that he had observed besides the "formalism" that Coleridge had cautioned him about. He was ordained deacon in 1815, and priest a year later. There are numerous anecdotes about candidates for Anglican orders being examined on the tennis courts and other nonecclesiastical places. It is curious that Keble was never examined at all.

---

[23]Principal Shairp, "John Keble and *The Christian Year*," *North British Review* 7 (July 1866): 239.

It is impossible to believe that Keble ever slipped into the completely relaxed life of many of his clerical contemporaries, but the description of Keble as a "saint" in the Church of England, largely because of his ministry at Hursley, brings with it an extraordinarily high standard of heroism. For the most part, Keble cannot be called heroic. There was nothing strenuous about his life as a clergyman. The letters record lengthy visits to friends and numerous visits to holiday centers in England. On one occasion he wrote to Coleridge about a visit to a newly married friend.

> I have not seen my old friend George Cornish for several years, and have never been at his house since he was married. This is my excuse for so unclerical a proceeding as leaving my three parishes for three or four Sundays in July.[24]

For a while at least Keble was a nonresident clergyman who interpreted his duties in a fairly relaxed manner. In another letter he records some of his activities.

> I am left [Keble wrote] at full liberty to draw pretty pictures of woodland walks and rides, social evenings and busy mornings with old and new friends at Hursley.[25]

The great business of clerical life was to get a good living, which meant for Keble scenery and agreeable companions. He commented on his brother's success at getting a good situation:

> . . . you must know that the Chancellor, through the kindness of Lord Stowell, has given Tom a pretty good living in this country, about 18 miles from Fairford, Bisley by name, and by description beggarly Bisley: there being about 6,000 people in the parish, many of them starving clothiers; 'tis an ugly place, but within reach of some pretty country.[26]

There are other letters that reveal a somewhat secular approach to the task of living in the lower levels of clerical life.

None of the above comments by Keble betray a vicious character, and Keble was certainly adequate to this task. At the same

---

[24]Keble to Coleridge, September 1817, CC.

[25]Ibid., 10 June 1815, CC.

[26]Ibid., 14 September 1816, CC.

time there is nothing that reminds a reader of the great Catholic saints (a claim that is made for Keble) or a high level of spiritual life. It is worth noting that Newman considered a good living the greatest "bribe" that the Church of England could offer to its clergy. In a manner of speaking, Keble fell for the bribe. When the offer of Hursley was made, with its beautiful house and very beautiful scenery, he accepted it without telling either Newman or Froude, remembering perhaps that he had pledged a year earlier never to accept such an appointment.

We have no way of knowing any of the details of Keble's early life as a priest, but in one of his earliest reviews for the *Quarterly* he made a series of comments on what was to be expected from the ideal preacher. The subject of Keble's review was a collection of sermons by an Anglican minister of the eighteenth century, William Alison. Keble briefly complained about "some metaphysical remarks in the sermon," but he concurred with Alison's judgment on the subject of Anglican doctrines.

> If the doctrines of our religion can be demonstrated upon the common principles of reason, to suppose that God could have made a miraculous revelation of them is absurd.[27]

Keble distinguished between natural religion and Christianity, but emphasized the reasonable appeal of Anglicanism. At the end of his essay he quoted another Anglican (Seeker) commentary on what a good preacher ought to do.

> Your business is, says he . . . "not to please or be admired, but to do good; to make men think not of your abilities, attainments or eloquence, but of the state of their own souls; and to fix them in the belief and practice of what will render them happy now and in eternity. Here then lay your foundation; and set before your people the lamentable condition of fallen man; the numerous actual sins by which they have made it worse; the redemption wrought for them by Jesus Christ; the nature and importance of true faith in him; their absolute need of the grace of the divine Spirit in order to obey his precepts. This will be addressing yourselves to them as Christian ministers ought to Christian hear-

---

[27][John Keble], "Alison's Sermons," *Quarterly Review* 14 (January 1816): 438.

ers. The holy scriptures will furnish you with matter for it abundantly. Short and plain reasonings, founded on their authority, will dart conviction into every mind; whereas if your doctrine and your speech be not that of their bibles; if you contradict or explain away, or pass over in silence, any thing taught there . . . they will be offended and quit you when they can. We have, in fact, lost many people to sectaries by not preaching in a manner sufficiently evangelical, and shall neither recover them from the extravagances into which they have run, nor keep more from going over to them but by returning to the right way, *declaring all the counsel of God.*"[28]

Yet there was another side of Keble's ministry at Hursley. Keble was not only involved as the spiritual leader of his flock, he had become one of the leading arbiters of the Church of England. James A. Froude, on the negative side, described the "mantle of authority" that Keble exercised over those who came to him for counsel on the Roman question as H. P. Liddon did when he remarked that men always waited for "word from Hursley"[29] when determining their course of duty. Keble's message was always the same: Do not leave the Church of England, no matter what bishops or the Privy Council might do or say about your belief in the Catholic teachings of the English church. Dr. Pusey once paid tribute to the influence of Keble on those who came to him for counsel.

I sent one to John Keble to get settled as to some Romeward unsettlement. He stayed a fortnight at Hursley. John Keble did not say a word of controversy, but loved. At the end of the time my friend told me that he was quite settled and could work heartily in the English Church.[30]

It is hard to determine who is being discussed in the Pusey letter, but it may have been the Bishop of Brechin ("The Scottish Pusey") who had been troubled by the unsettlements in the church and

---

[28]Ibid., 443.

[29]Quoted in Battiscombe, *John Keble,* 305.

[30]*Spiritual Letters of E. B. Pusey,* ed. James Johnson and William Newbolt (London: Longman's, Green, & Co., 1898) 289.

had gone to Keble for help. After he left Hursley, Keble wrote to Pusey,

> Our friend had been with me since Friday evening. . . . we had some more talk; all confirming me in the impression that it is a longing for rest rather than intellectual conviction that Rome is right which is working on him. I hope he was a little more comfortable when he left us . . . promising to do so I desired him; which was to treat the haunting thought as simply a distress. . . . I also begged him to think of the terrible consequence of such moves.[31]

This was Keble's message for his contemporaries. The desire for religious certitude was probably a sign of some moral evil, and a good Anglican would never make such demands upon his church or himself. Keble was not always successful with those who were unsettled, yet it is very significant that those who did go over to Rome noted that Keble's influence kept them so long in the English church. None of the converts, moreover, ever took a hard line with Keble in their controversial writings against the Catholic claims of the English church. The blame and condemnations were always directed against Dr. Pusey, Keble's associate and friend.

Hursley was a kind of shrine for Catholic-minded Anglicans, and without the influence of Keble the list of converts might have been much greater than it was. In that series of visitors to Hursley, Keble preached a version of Catholicism that was known to relatively few. His idea was that every church has problems and scandals and that those of Rome were at least equal to those of the English church. As he wrote to one friend,

> One has to satisfy oneself, sufficiently for practice, what the judgment of Christendom is. It makes no difference in principle, whether the process is easier or harder. The Roman plan seems to me an unreal endeavor to evade by a certain form of words a responsibility which cannot be evaded. Can any one doubt after all, that J. H. N. and H. E. M. are taking on themselves a most heavy responsibility: I should say greater, but at least as great, as if they had stayed with us.[32]

---

[31]John Keble to E. B. Pusey, 14 June 1864, in Keble-Pusey Correspondence, vol. 4, Pusey House, Oxford.

[32]Ibid., 13 May 1859, vol. 3.

The converts, according to Keble, were answerable for everything that was taught or permitted by Rome—worship of the saints, transubstantiation, (perhaps) the sanction of lying as found in Liguori—and the innovations were at least equal to various imperfections in the English church. Following this line of argument, Keble insisted that the safest way for Anglicans was to remain in the church in which they had been born and educated.

Keble's Politics

One of the neglected aspects of Keble's intellectual development is a life-long interest in political affairs as they affected the Church of England. The popular image of Keble as a retiring, self-effacing type does not readily coalesce with the idea of a political clergyman, or one who spent a great deal of energy in addressing political questions in his comments, pamphlets, and sermons. For the most part, Keble's biographers, and historians of the Oxford Movement, have interpreted his life as exclusively spiritual and "other worldly." According to this view, Keble and his friends had no concern for the great social issues of their day.

John Keble was a conservative in both a good and bad sense. As for the latter interpretation, there was a certain amount of "looking out for number one" in his approach to political affairs of the church. His early sermons illustrate a strong hostility to every form of political liberalism—"rebellion" as he called it—and he extended his denunciations of the rebellious mentality to those who expressed any sympathy for liberalism. His argument was that no one would express sympathy towards murder or adultery or those who practiced it, but it was somewhat fashionable to sympathize with rebellion, in direct contradiction to the mandates of St. Paul and the Prayer Book, which clearly instructed the ordinary Christian in the lesson of obedience.

In later sermons Keble defended the alliance of church and state and the rightful debt that the state owed to the church: The endowments of the church, he insisted, should be as handsome as possible, "whatever else appears to be neglected."

On the positive side of Keble's "Toryism," Keble did have an enormous respect for the established order and the traditions that sustained that order. As Newman wrote in his *Apologia,*

Keble was a man who guided himself and formed his judgments ... by authority. What he hated instinctively was heresy, insubordination, resistance to things established, claims of independence.[33]

Keble was a Tory in the style of Dr. Johnson; Keble's creed was the "creed of Oxford," a blend of philosophic idealism and self-interest. In his conservatism, Keble was the heir of the Elizabethan settlement—"The Elizabethan World picture," as the Reformation Toryism was described. God had appointed to every man a specific place, and it was morally wrong to oppose that divinely established order.

There are many illustrations of Keble's conservatism throughout his writings, but it is noteworthy that the *Quarterly,* with its numerous Tory writers, should have allowed Keble to do the review of Chateaubriand's *Monarchy.*[34] Keble's "lesson" in that essay was that political liberalism, no less than monarchy, had its own form of tyranny, a lesson that he preached more rigorously to John Taylor Coleridge.

Nor has there been any moment in my memory when the Church of England, as an Establishment, seems in so much jeopardy: however Church and State and all together have been brought through so much worse scrapes that it would be most unworthy to despond ... but I really think matters are in a train to give either us or the next generation an opportunity of practicing your lessons and St. Paul's teaching of non-resistance and acquiescence: which I suppose will apply as well to the subjects of a liberalistic as to those of a monarchical tyranny. . . . such an example would do infinitely more good than the continuance of our temporal advantages.[35]

And such was the argument of Keble's early political thought. Every government presented the threat of tyranny; but the danger was even greater when a government had set itself up in de-

---

[33]*Apologia Pro Vita Sua,* 14th ed., 290.

[34]John Griffin, "John Keble and *The Quarterly Review," Review of English Studies* 29 (November 1978): 454-55.

[35]Keble to Coleridge, June 1827, CC.

fiance of moral law. However archaic Keble's appeal to the idea of an ordered universe might appear to ourselves, it was the most traditional aspect of Keble's thought.

In 1827 Keble used the word *erastian* for the first time in his correspondence. He applied the word to Sir Robert Peel for his sudden shift of loyalties on the issue of Catholic Emancipation. The word, then and now, is extremely rare in Anglican usage, and Keble may have taken it from one of Milton's prose works. It does not appear in Johnson's *Dictionary,* and while the concept that erastianism represents—state control of the church—was well-known to the English and for the most part agreed to without dissent, the idea that the church was an extension of the state suddenly began to bother Keble. The Oxford Movement was the principal result of his irritation at the idea that the Church of England had no real existence apart from its connections with the state, that it was a "mere Parliamentary church" as he remarked in "National Apostasy."

The politics of the Oxford Movment were a form of quiescent radicalism, a passive compliance with the state's efforts to disestablish the church. In Keble's case the radicalism was short-lived. His basic irritation, before and after the Oxford Movement, was at the idea of non-Anglicans having any say in the spiritual affairs of the Church of England. Yet the idea of separating from the state was also short-lived. In little more than a year after the Movement had started, Keble had settled into what Newman once called the "hollow Toryism" that was brought on at the Reformation.

In the years after Newman's conversion erastianism became an even more important element in the lives of high-churchmen. State trials of Anglo-Catholic doctrines were increasingly common after 1850, but Keble and his contemporaries gave up the word *erastianism* and the radical solution to that heresy. In almost every trial there was a flurry of petitions and pamphlet writing that seemed to salve the conscience of the Anglo-Catholic party, but the earlier radicalism was gone forever. No one ever mentioned giving up his living or his professional chair, and Keble himself seems to have given up all political interests after 1850.

The Final Years, 1845-1866

When Cardinal Newman gave his letters from Keble to Keble College, he added a note of explanation for the numerous blottings that he had added to these letters.

> In the Letters which follow I have made erasures, which may seem strange and arbitrary, unless I say something to account for them. Let me observe then that dear John Keble's heart was too tender and his religious senses too keen for him not to receive serious injury to his spirits and mental equilibrium by the long succession of trials, in which his place in the Oxford Movement involved him.[36]

Newman mentioned a number of events that had been especially disturbing to Keble—all occurring in the final years of the Oxford Movement—but his comments have been interpreted as an extension of his own instability at the time.[37]

Newman had an advantage over most of Keble's biographers: he had actually known Keble and read the letters any material was erased. The other person who knew Keble, J. T. Coleridge, implicitly verified the accuracy of Newman's portrait because Keble's letters to Coleridge do appear very gloomy. It has been mentioned in only one biography of Keble, but it appears that Keble considered leaving the Church of England long before Newman did.

> The contingency that I contemplate, a very dreary one, but such an one as I, ought not to think it strange if I incur it, is, not going to Rome, but being driven out of all communion whatever. I cannot hide it from myself that two Prelates have distinctly denied an article of the Apostles' Creed . . . and that while no notice is taken of them, attempts are being made in Oxford, and in many Dioceses at once, to enforce a view equivalent to theirs.[38]

There are several relevant points that might be made about Keble's outlook in 1841. The first is obvious from the above. He was

---

[36]Dessain and Gornall, *Letters and Diaries,* 28:292.

[37]Battiscombe, *John Keble,* 234.

[38]Coleridge, *Memoir,* 299.

perhaps the first of the Tractarians to actually mention leaving the Church of England, and in 1841 at least he was praising Newman for his steadfast loyalty to the national church; yet in 1845 he put the rumor into circulation that Newman had not been a loyal Anglican for five years.[39] A second point might also be remarked on from the above. Keble never considered the Roman Catholic Church as much more than a doctrinal and moral sham. Those scholars who have argued that Keble and the other Anglo-Catholics were ecumenical in their positive attitude towards Rome have neglected much evidence that contradicts such an assertion.

The final point about the letter, Keble's prospect of being "out of all communion whatever," is, I would suggest, the dominant motif of his last twenty years, except that he did not actually leave the national church. The scholars who have praised Keble's "loyalty" to the Church of England have neglected his frequent quarrels with the bishops, state, fellow clergy, and even his fellow Anglo-Catholics—a course of opposition that argues for a loyalty perhaps only to himself.

The best example of Keble's increasingly independent stance in religious matters is to be found at the end of the Gorham trial. Richard Gorham was a low-churchman who denied the doctrine of baptismal regeneration (the doctrine that baptism is essential for membership in the church) and who, because of his denial, was refused a living in the diocese of Henry Phillpotts, Bishop of Exeter. Having been denied the living, Gorham took his case to the Privy Council, a secular court set up for ecclesiastical cases. Eventually Gorham won; the disputed doctrine was declared to be an "open question" in the church of England.

After the verdict was given, the Anglo-Catholics signed a petition that declared that if the verdict were not rejected by the church, "it would forfeit its authority as a divine teacher." There was only a limited support for the petition, but one of the leaders of the Anglo-Catholics remarked that if the petition did not work,

---

[39]Keble to Coleridge, June 1845, CC; see also John Griffin, "The Anglican Response to Newman's Conversion," *Faith and Reason* 3 (June 1977): 17-34.

"we just join the church of Rome." Keble responded, "If the church of England were to fail, it should be found in my parish." Keble, I maintain, meant exactly what he said: It was his judgment on church matters that was important, even if everyone else—bishops, fellow-clergy, courts, and laity—disagreed. This was the position he maintained for the rest of his life.[40]

In various letters and publications from 1841 through the end of his life, Keble did sometimes set himself up as the only witness to English Catholic orthodoxy. It would be hard to think of a single act of charity towards those who could not bring themselves to follow his advice, and his writings and remarks against Rome increased as his problems with the English church increased. Keble was especially opposed to Rome's "worship of the B.V.M" and its doctrines of infallibility and transubstantiation. But he also opposed the English bishops at almost every turn after Newman's conversion. In one especially heated letter to the Bishop of Winchester he noted that "the truth might be held by a remnant only."[41]

In his comments to an Anglo-Catholic friend, Keble noted that "truth must ever be unpopular." If opposition is the test of truth, Keble was the one exponent of Catholic orthodoxy in the world. His views on Mary, while different from those of Rome, were very different from those of even his most intimate friends. He opposed the doctrine of transubstantiation throughout his life, and yet he also differed from Pusey in his version of the Eucharist (though I do not think that either the views of Pusey or Keble could ever be defined). He was sympathetic to the idea of confession, but did not push its use after his patron refused to allow it at Hursley; yet he was also uncomfortable with some of Pusey's efforts as editor of the Roman confessional manuals. The clue to Keble's position, intellectual and religious, in the last twenty years is to be found in his advocacy of Private Judgment—the Protestant idea that the individual is his own priest and must de-

---

[40]Edmund Purcell, *Life of Cardinal Manning*, 2 vols. (London: Macmillan Co., 1906) 1:254, 528-29.

[41]Keble to Bishop of Winchester, February 1850, vol. 2, CC.

cide for himself which doctrines he accepts and which he does not. Because of Rome's denial of Private Judgment (among many other reasons), Keble determined he could never go over. Such an exercise of the intellect on doctrinal matters was a "responsibility that cannot be evaded."[42]

In the midst of his many difficulties with the Church of England, Keble kept up the steady warfare against Rome and the prospect of persons following Newman's example. While defending his own exercise of Private Judgment, he virtually denied it to every one else. The converts of 1845 and later were stigmatized as "beacons"—persons who would not listen to the voice of their elders. Still it might be remembered that Keble's success rate with potential converts—"perverts" as they were known in Anglo-Catholic circles—was not that great. Several of his closest friends went over, and each was then regarded as "practically dead."[43]

In the years after 1845 there was an increasing isolation of Keble's religious views, yet he maintained a close friendship with Pusey and Coleridge. Pusey pushed Catholic practices and doctrines as far as he thought was possible and, while Keble referred to him as a "Puseyite of the deepest dye,"[44] he did not share all of Pusey's religious views and practices. The friendship with Coleridge is more difficult to describe. Coleridge, as a public figure, was more "Protestant" than anything else. Certainly he was more opposed to Rome and "Romish" practices than even Keble, but the cementing factor in the relationship of both men—an Anglo-Catholic and a Protestant to Keble—is probably to be found in Keble's increased reluctance to engage in any form of religious discussion. In perhaps this last meeting with Newman, he is reported to have said, "If the Church of Rome is the true church, I do not know it; I do not know it."[45] The doctrine that he was in-

---

[42]Keble-Pusey Correspondence, February 1851, vol. 2, Pusey House, Oxford.

[43]Keble to Coleridge, 16 October 1845, CC.

[44]Harry P. Liddon, *Life of E. B. Pusey,* 4 vols. (London: Macmillan and Co., 1898) 3:283.

[45]Ibid., 4:257-58.

voking for himself was the doctrine of Invincible Ignorance: persons who act in good faith are not answerable for the correctness of their views.

Keble's two closest friends, after Newman's departure, were Coleridge and Pusey, though Charlotte Yonge, the novelist, moved into that group during the final years of Keble's life. She notes that in Keble's final years he acquired a fierce dislike of all religious controversy and that he rejoiced in the doctrine of purgatory, as almost the final gesture of his independent but troubled spirit.

Keble died in 1866, six weeks before his wife Charlotte. His final thirty years were spent at Hursley, ministering to his flock and to his invariably ailing wife. There were no children, and I do not think that the wife's illness has ever been explained. The marriage, however, like the vicarage at Hursley, was not a part of the original idealism of 1833 in which he envisioned an independent church and an impoverished and celibate clergy.

Plans for some kind of memorial to John Keble were made immediately after his funeral. The result of these efforts by Pusey and others was Keble College, opened in 1876 as a tribute to the faith and loyalty of John Keble.

Conclusion

What emerges from this sketch of Keble's life is a generally different portrait of the man and his family background. Keble was not born into a high-church family, and the poetry of *The Christian Year* should not be considered as part of the Oxford Movement. Until he was forty, Keble was closer to the Liberal (anti-dogmatic) Protestant tradition than his biographers have realized. When the conflicts over the Tractarian ideology began, he retreated to his parish at Hursley and to a form of "Donatism" that sustained his later years.

Given the variety of religious views, and the many differences that he expressed between his views and those of even his narrow circle of Oxford friends, Keble moved into an increasingly isolated position in his religious outlook and teachings. Yet if he was not exactly the confessor of ancestral Anglo-Catholic doctrine, he was at least a far more original and complex religious thinker than has been commonly realized. Keble always maintained a severe independent in reaching conclusions on religious doctrines, and if he was occasionally belligerent in defending those doctrines, he was at least far more "creative" in his approach to the traditions of the Church of England.

Chapter II

Keble's Literary Criticism

Keble began his work as a literary critic in 1814 writing, in the course of thirty years as an occasional reviewer, a dozen essays on various subjects in the usual style of nineteenth-century reviewing: The book review came to be an essay on the subject of the book under review. In his collection of published and unpublished essays, there are several expressly devoted to literary subjects, and in the course of doing this study, I have found two other essays that should be added to the list. His early work was published in the conservative, Protestant journals of the time: *Quarterly Review, British Critic* (not an Anglo-Catholic journal in the early nineteenth century), and *British Magazine.*

The politics and religion of the three journals are a reflection of Keble's own disposition on both subjects, but he broke off a budding relationship with the *Quarterly* for religious reasons in 1816. (The *Quarterly* had suddenly become too concerned with "orthodoxy.") By the time he wrote his final literary essay, Keble was an Anglo-Catholic. His new belief that the Church of England was to be regarded as a branch of the "Catholic, apostolic church" gave a sudden twist to his reading of Sir Walter Scott.

The essays on literature have one outstanding feature that might be noted: Keble's meaning is always clear. The reader does not have to agree with Keble to appreciate his constant clarity of exposition and his general condemnation of obscurity in poetry and literary theory. Keble, moreover, was strongly opposed to any speculations about literature that took the reader away from the actual texts; thus, his own essays are filled with references to the text being discussed and ample citations from the poetry.

One important characteristic of his essays on literature is the general "kindness" (for want of a better word) of the reviewer towards the material, and its author, that is being discussed. A reader of popular Victorian reviews will appreciate the rareness of such a quality in the press at a time when reviewing often seemed to take on a punitive quality. And even when Keble was distinctly unhappy with some facet of the work under discussion, he always managed to temper his commentary with good manners.

A further aspect of Keble's literary essays can be found in his frequent challenge to established literary critics, including Aristotle, Dr. Johnson, and a host of usually unnamed critics. Above all, there is a certain anti-intellectualism in his distaste for all elaborate forms of criticism, theory, and analysis. It was Keble's belief that the more we claim to understand a poem, the less we appreciate it; but Keble also disliked any kind of commentary that interfered with the reader's own perception of the poem.

Keble is usually regarded as a Romantic critic because of his insistence on the emotional or affective aspects of literature. It is true that throughout his work we can trace a deliberate break with some of the ideas set forth in Aristotle's *Poetics* and Dr. Johnson's *Lives of the English Poets,* especially Keble's dislike for the idea of poetry as "imitation" and Johnson's condemnation of the idea of religious poetry. Yet there are important links between Keble's work and the Neo-Classic tradition that should be noted. Keble was suspicious of any claims to being different by the poet, and he insisted that the ideas of the poet should be those of common humanity; that is, poetry must be reasonable in its themes. Throughout much of his early criticism, Keble constantly appealed to the common sensibilities and experiences of humanity. Cosmic or "metaphysical" speculations by the poet about himself or the world were condemned. For Keble, good poetry was never egotistical or metaphysical.

The Essays on Literature

Keble's first literary essay was a review of Edward Copleston's *Praelectiones Academicae* ("Academic Lectures on Poetry"), a series of lectures on art and poetry that Copleston, a friend of Keble, had given as Professor of Poetry in 1813 at Oxford. As the title suggests, the lectures were originally given in Latin, and Keble's quotations from the text are given without a translation.[1] Keble's review-essay is almost as broad in its survey of art, poetry, and literary criticism as the text it reviews. The basic thrust of his essay is that of praise for Copleston's part in breaking English literary theory from the "shackles of French taste," which had never been really popular in England. Criticism had once been a "useful handmaid, if not worthy coadjutor of moral philosophy," but in the early part of the eighteenth century the French had degraded literary and artistic theory into a "cold, unmeaning formalist process." Copleston was congratulated for his awareness that "the business of criticism" was to "enumerate rather than demonstrate" the characteristics of literary taste, for the basic axioms of criticism were "drawn from the feelings, not the reason." One of the distinctive marks of Copleston's achievement was its candid avowal of the primacy of feelings in the evaluation of a poem. The author was "not ashamed of avowing a feeling, without assigning a direct argument for it."[2]

Having praised the book for this quality, Keble pointed out what he thought was a central weakness in the author's argument. Copleston had not troubled to define the distinctive pleasures of poetry: "He who gives most pleasure [Copleston said] supposing the source of that pleasure poetical, is the best poet." Keble urged that there should be finer discrimination between the kinds of feeling that poetry could and should generate. The great pleasure of poetry was to be found in "the graces of the form" used

---

[1]"Copleston's *Praelectiones Academicae*," first published in the *British Critic,* 1814; reprinted in *Occasional Papers and Reviews,* ed. Harry P. Liddon (Oxford: James Parker & Co., 1877) 148-62; all references will be to the Liddon edition.

[2]Ibid., 148-49.

by the poet; and while there was no specific formula for the causes "both of beauty and poetry," there was a moral law that the best poetry reflected.

> It is to the awakening of some moral or religious feeling, not by direct instruction (that is the office of moral theology) but by way of association that we refer all poetical pleasures.[3]

Keble's point of reference in the above was the common experience of all mankind: the greatest pleasures that life offered were moral, and the task of the poet was to illustrate indirectly the common, moral sensibilities of mankind. The greatest poetry was always, though usually in an indirect sense, moral in its affirmation of "knowing right from wrong." But the poet never preached. His purpose was to express "ideas and language calculated to raise religious and moral associations."[4]

Having argued that the artistic response is essentially moral in its character, Keble described the importance of the imagination to the reader: " . . . the mind is excited to fill up the picture [or poem] itself." The artist's role was to supply the outline of the object; for example, the pleasures of art were not in "the perception of likeness" (Aristotle's idea), but rather in stimulus that the work of art became to the imagination of the reader. The pleasures of art were emotional and not necessarily rational.

> All the pleasures of poetry . . . imply the embodying of something visionary, the presenting something absent, the bettering of something imperfect: their very being lies in the consciousness of some such operation. Now what (expecting a mind thoroughly diseased and depraved, wherein imagination and reason too are slaves of the body) what can tend more strongly to make man feel his own dignity; to disencumber him of earthly affections, and lift him nearer what he once was, and what he may be again, than the exercise and invigoration of a power so totally independent of material things, so much at variance with the senses as this is? If, then, all the honest pleasures of the imagination have this high kindred, and if we may boldly exclude as unpoetical such as are corrupt and sensual, what hinders but that the poetry of the

---

[3]Ibid., 150.
[4]Ibid., 152.

imagination, as well as that of the heart, he owned to have its beginning and end is in religious and moral association.[5]

According to Keble, the imagination was a moral faculty; and in
this sense alone can Keble be considered as didactic. As we shall
see, his opposition to direct moral instruction in art grew stronger
in his later essays—an opposition that led him into serious conflict with a poet (Wordsworth) he later admired very much.

Keble's second essay on literature was a critical review of
Wordsworth's first two volumes of poetry and his "New Preface
and a Supplemental Essay." The essay has not been noticed by
Keble scholars as one of his writings, nor was it included in the
collection of his papers edited by H. Liddon in 1877. Even J. T.
Coleridge did not mention the essay, though Keble noted its com-
pletion in a letter to him:

> My Wordsworth is now quite ready, + shall be sent up in good
> time i.e., by the end of the month, if not wanted sooner, but by a
> post's notice at any time.[6]

The essay on Wordsworth was not published until the end of 1815.
Keble, perhaps out of a sense of embarrassment, did not refer directly to the essay in his later letters.

The essay is an important piece of early Wordsworthian criticism in its clarity and perception. At this time Keble was not un-
qualified in his admiration of Wordsworth's poetry, and the
ultimate effect of this essay is rather a strong indictment of some
of the central concerns of Wordsworth's poetry and criticism. The
essay might be read as a direct attack on Wordsworth's poems and
literary theory.

Wordsworth's poetry was "directly the reverse of simple,"[7]
though the poet was obviously a gifted person with a "true feeling
for poetry." Keble praised the poet for his correct attitude towards poetry and the personal qualities that he reflected in some
of his poems. Wordsworth had all the necessary qualities to become a great poet including,

---

[5]Ibid., 158.

[6]Keble to Coleridge, 10 April 1815, CC.

[7]"Wordsworth's Poetry," *Quarterly Review* 14 (January 1816): 224.

. . . evaluation of sentiment—tenderness of heart—the truest
sensibilities for the beauties of nature—combined with extraordinary fervor of imagination, and a most praiseworthy love of
simplicity both in thought and language.[8]

But with all of these gifts, Wordsworth had not yet achieved any
kind of popularity; and Keble's essay was directed at the reasons
for Wordsworth's failure to capture the popular imagination.

Keble first questioned the veiled egotism of the poet's opinion
that his own fate was the fate "in all ages . . . of poets greatly en-
dowed with originality of genius." According to Keble, the answer for Wordsworth's failure was much easier. Wordsworth was
always "straining" after some form of originality that exceeded
"plain good sense." In particular, Keble found fault in Wordsworth's use of poetry for "metaphysical instruction," arguing that
poetry could not easily bear such a burden. The common reader,
moreover, did not read poetry in order to be instructed in religion
or philosophy.[9]

Keble defended popular taste in its judgment against Wordsworth's merits as a poet; and he noted that the tone of Wordsworth's prose did nothing to help the poet achieve a wider reading.
It was, Keble said,

. . . distinguished by a tone which, in any other person, we should
feel ourselves called upon to treat with some little severity. For
a writer to protest that he *prides* himself upon the disapproba-
tion of his contemporaries, and consider it as an evidence of the
originality of his genius . . . is whimsical enough, to say the least
of it; but Mr. Wordsworth ought, at all events, to be consistent
with himself; and since he derives so many suspicious assur-
ances from the opposition which his opinions have met with, he
should speak with a little more moderation of those by whom he
happens to be opposed. He should remember, moreover, that the
public, and those who profess to be organs of the public voice in
these matters, have at least as much right to dislike *his* poetical
taste, as he has to dislike theirs.[10]

[8]Ibid., 201.
[9]Ibid., 204-205.
[10]Ibid., 202-203.

Keble's comments on Wordsworth's pose of indifference to his readers and his belief that such an indifference was a proof of personal merit strike me as unanswerable, and suggest an affinity with the appeal of Dr. Johnson to the common reader and the relationship that should exist between the reader and the poet. The reader should be able to respond to the art and ideas of the poet as if they were his own.

Keble continued his challenge to Wordsworth's general ideas about the poet and his relationship to his audience by attacking one of Wordsworth's most celebrated criticisms—the comments on Thomas Gray's sonnet "Richard West," a poem that Wordsworth had declared to be artificial. Keble thought the sonnet was excellent because it was "addressed to our reason" and "perfectly intelligible," a quality that Wordsworth sorely lacked. The poet was always concerned with a "delineation of himself and his own peculiar feelings."

The word *peculiar* should be noted, for it is the basis of one of Keble's most trenchant criticisms of Wordsworth and (implicitly) much Romantic poetry. In the use of such a word, Keble suggests a fundamental dissent from the idea that the poet was in any way different from the rest of humanity. The complaint that Wordsworth's poems were too much concerned with the personal feelings of the poet was at once practical and theoretical. A poet should therefore "express himself as other men express themselves" with a concern for the common emotions of mankind, exactly the principle that Keble and his friends had followed in their own writing of poetry. The great failing of Wordsworth was that he expressed himself too freely (he had no reserve) and that his feelings were "tuned much too high for the sobriety of truth."[11]

Keble, then, was not an early admirer of Wordsworth's poetry, and the scholars who find parallels between the *Lyrical Ballads* and *The Christian Year* are unfair to both poets. There was of course a change of heart or judgment on Keble's side, begin-

---

[11]Ibid., 205; the word *peculiar* came to be the later Tractarian description of the Evangelicals, and it suggests any unrestrained emotions or personal revelations.

ning perhaps in 1816, when Keble met Wordsworth. After that meeting, Keble praised Wordsworth the man and noted that he had avoided all poetical and "metaphysical" discussion during their conversion.[12]

There was a break of ten years in Keble's relations with the *Quarterly,* and it was not until 1825 that he published another essay, this time on a subject that was obviously congenial to the poet-critic, "Sacred Poetry." In this essay Keble offered a detailed inquiry into the materials and history of religious poetry in England, and the lengthy essay might be read as an extended preface to his forthcoming book of poems, *The Christian Year.* In a nominal sense at least, Keble's essay was a review of a recently published collection of religious poems, Josiah Conder's *The Star in the East and Other Poems.*

Keble praised the "unpretending tone" of Conder's work and suggested that the poetry had "internal evidence" to the effect that it was never written for publication. Keble explained that a critic must exercise restraint in his comments on such poetry, for such poems,

> . . . if they appear to be written with any degree of sincerity and earnestness, we naturally shrink from treating them merely as literary efforts. To interrupt the current of a reader's sympathy in such a case . . . is to disturb him almost in a devotional exercise.[13]

Conder's work passed the above tests in that he did not seem to deliberately place himself in the role of "poet" or seek to draw attention to himself.

There were some weaknesses in his poems, however; one of the central poems in the colllection, "The Star in the East," with its use of blank, dramatic verse had a "less pleasing character" than the other poems in the collection: the inflated quality of most blank verse gave it a "deficiency of truth" in presentation.

---

[12]Keble to Coleridge, 20 May 1815, CC.

[13][John Keble], "Sacred Poetry," *Quarterly Review* 32 (June 1825): 211-32; reprinted in Liddon, *Occasional Papers and Reviews,* 81.

There were other weaknesses in Conder's poetry. Keble noted that the poet had an unrealistic sense of the world and that his ambition of converting the world to the ideals of Christianity was impossible. The world would probably never be converted, and even if it were, it "would be very little changed for the better." Keble's remark on the theme of one of Conder's poems might seem curious or cynical unless we remember that he lived in a country that was by declaration Christian. Keble's response to Conder was based on his observation that England had been very little changed for the better because of its official profession of the Christian religion. A further aspect of his commentary can be found in his general criticism (throughout his work) of all ambitions and professions that seemed too much for fallen humanity.

Keble's comments on Conder's poetry are derived from the same motif that informed his criticism of Wordsworth's poems. Both poets suffered from an inability to present truth that could be appreciated by most of humanity. Wordsworth was limited by his overabundant sense of self, and Conder by his lack of experience with the objects he was describing. Both poets were "wanting in truth," a quality as essential to "the higher kinds of poetical beauty, as to philosophy, or history itself."

Keble never did actually define truth; nor did he clarify the kind of philosophy that he was appealing to in his assertion that poetry must possess the same truth as philosophy. But he seems to have meant the common experience of man as opposed to the "far-off" or "deluding ambition" of those who came to be obsessed by some ideal beyond human expectations. What is most interesting in the Keble essay, however, is the element of praise that he bestows on the domestic poems of Conder. "The Poor Man's Hymn," for example, was a poem in celebration of the particular contentments of the life of the poor, who were happy with their lives because they knew that Christ was poor. One of Keble's most consistent ideas about poverty, and even more so about politics, was that the poor were content (or should be content) with their position in life. Conder's poems on domestic matters were "drawn from life." It never occurred to Keble that such poetry might be as deficient in empirical truth as "metaphysical" poetry.

The basic ideal was the avoidance of all affectation. Great poetry was characterized by simplicity of statement, and it was always a reflection of the general experiences of mankind. With a glance at "the most vicious of all styles, the style of Mr. Leigh Hunt and his miserable followers," Keble illustrated his ideal of poetic beauty by an analysis of the Psalms. The Hebrew poet was indifferent towards any concern for originality, or "what is technically called effect." The true poet, especially the sacred poet, wrote to unburden his mind, not for "the sake of writing" itself or to make a reputation for himself. He loved his subject and worked to ennoble it; but he was not attracted to the idea of being a poet.[14]

To illustrate his idea, Keble compared the poetry of Cowper and Burns. Burns was "overflowing with the love of nature," while Cowper was not really interested in nature, but wrote about it only "in default of some more congenial happiness." In making his case for the superiority of Burns's work Keble cited one of Burns's love poems (described as a "pastoral chant") and commented on the poet's "instinctive attachment to his subject" as the source of his superiority. It is especially interesting to notice that Keble had no complaint about some of the raciness in Burns's poems, though he addressed the question of obscenity in literature in his *Lectures*. (His later comments were that the reader who had the virtues of "modesty, simplicity, and purity" could benefit from even the most "tasteless" writers.)

At almost the conclusion of his essay on religious poetry, Keble made mention of one of the ideas that came to dominate the later *Lectures:* the idea of reserve (though Keble did not use the the word), or concealment of the self through art. The great poets did not display personal feelings for public attention, an idea that Keble found in Wordsworth's "Stock Dove" from which he quoted the lines:

> He should sing 'of love with silence blending,
> Slow to begin, yet never ending,
> Of serious faith and inward glee.

---

[14]Ibid., 86-88.

Keble took a stand against many of the more popular forms of English Romantic poetry; and his religious views are very like his views about poetry. Both should be characterized by an inward joy and an external restraint. With this growing concern with an idea of reserve in art and religion, Keble reflected almost the whole of his experience and reading. The Greeks and Romans had practiced such restraint, and Keble's Oxford background and its ideal of the gentleman who "never speaks of himself except when compelled" contributed to the formation of the idea of reserve in art. Poetry should be "fervent, yet sober; awful, but engaging; neither wild and passionate, nor light and airy." Such moderation was essential if the poet was to imitate the modest reserve that was practiced by the author of Christianity himself. Keble concluded his description of the religious poet with these comments:

> ... in addition to the ordinary difficulties of poetry, all these things are essential to the success of the Christian lyricist—if what he sets before us must be true in substance, and in manner marked by a noble simplicity and confidence in that truth, by a sincere attachment to it, and entire familiarity with it—then we need not wonder that so few should have become eminent in this branch of their art.[15]

It is no surprise that Keble passed over so many of the poets that we now regard as classics in English Christian literature. Simplicity was essential to the religious poet, and even the most devoted admirer of the metaphysical poets would scarcely allow that they were simple.

Poetry was not an instrument for philosophic speculation or direct religious instruction, and it emphatically was not the vehicle to suggest doubt in its basic subject matter—the existence or attributes of God. Keble's insistence on the absence of doubt in religious poetry is a major clue to the apparent simplemindedness of his own work, but Keble had an ample literary tradition for his own beliefs and ideals: Chaucer, Spenser, and Milton are poets of Christian confidence.

---

[15]Ibid., 91.

Following his discussion of the various qualities of religious poetry—restraint, simplicity, and confidence—Keble addressed himself to the question of whether it was possible to write religious poetry in the first place, the last issue in the essay on religious poetry and one of the reasons for my suggestion that the essay might be regarded as a kind of preface to the forthcoming volume of poems.

The question of the possibility of religious poetry invariably gets around to the comments of Dr. Johnson in his "Life of Waller," in which Johnson remarked that "contemplative poetry or the intercourse between God and the human soul, cannot be poetical." Keble disagreed, but gently pointed to Johnson's religious disposition as the source of his judgment on religious poetry. Dr. Johnson was one of those who might be numbered

> . . . among serious, but somewhat fearful, believers . . . who start
> at the very mention of Sacred poetry, as though poetry were . . .
> a profane amusement.[16]

And not withstanding Keble's high admiration for certain aspects of Johnson's criticism, he believed that Johnson's fearful and negative outlook on the human condition made him less responsive to the general experience of mankind in religious matters. For Keble, most believers responded to Christianity in the spirit of joy, rather than fear.

Yet there were points of agreement between Johnson and Keble in their response to metaphysical poetry. Both men were critical of the easy familiarity that some of the metaphysical poets exhibited towards God and other sacred subjects and, in Keble's case especially, the doubt they seemed to cast on their subject matter. Still, Johnson's assertion that the issue of religion (man's salvation) was so serious a matter that the use of poetry's techniques (wit, imagination, and intelligence) was out of place in the awesome burden of saving one's soul went completely counter to Keble's ideology. Poetry, Keble argued, affirmed man's innately moral nature; and in its appeal to Nature (flower, landscapes, etc.), it also affirmed man's ability to discern right from wrong.

---

[16]Ibid., 92.

In its address to man's aspirations toward the infinite, poetry reflected the providential origins and destiny of mankind. Good poetry could hardly escape being religious.

It is not a great surprise that Keble had little taste for some of the better known poets of the seventeenth century. Even his deep admiration of George Herbert strikes me as an exception to his critical theory, instead of its confirmation. Poets who reflected the tension, ambiguity, and paradox of the Christian experience damaged the cause of Christianity by throwing the reader into a similar perplexity. The reader's attention, moreover, was directed to the poet and to figuring out his meaning, thus, he was deprived of those joyous associations that were the basis of the Christian experience.

The essay ends with a brief history of religious poetry in England, but the discussion includes only those poets who had shown a major interest in religion in their work. Spenser was the greatest of these.

> To Spenser . . . the English reader must revert, as being, preeminently, the sacred poet of his country: as most likely, in every way to answer the purposes of his art; especially in an age of excitation and refinement . . . and so exactly fulfilling what he has himself declared to be "the general end of all his book"—"to fashion a gentleman, or a noble person, in virtuous and gentle discipline."[17]

The ideal of a gentleman that Keble invoked in the above, which Newman was to describe later in his *Idea of a University,* has been attacked by modern scholars as tepid and unattractive, but Keble was giving utterance to one of the great Oxford traditions in his commentary: the gentleman was a man of sensitivity, tolerance, and sympathy, one "who never talked of himself except when compelled." However, there is an important difference between Newman and Keble that should be noted briefly. For Keble, so far as we can tell from the above comments on Spenser and from other comments in the *Lectures,* the "gentleman" was a moral figure in himself. Newman suggested that, while the idea of being one "who

---

[17]Ibid., 98.

never inflicts pain" was the highest level to which unaided human nature could aspire, it was not in itself a moral ideal. A gentleman might be damned if he ignored the higher virtues of faith, hope, and charity. Nevertheless, the formation of the gentleman was the social result of education. Keble went further than Newman in his praise of the ideal, but he furnished one more "proof" for his assertion that Spenser was the greatest religious poet that England has produced: Spenser used allegory to conceal his inmost feelings about himself and his religion.

There is one final essay on a literary topic—Keble's review of the *Memoirs of the Life of Sir Walter Scott* (1838), written for the now Anglo-Catholic journal *The British Critic*. By the time Keble came to write his essay, both the Oxford Movement and the *Lectures on Poetry* were well underway, and some of the religious ideology of the Anglo-Catholic revival interfered with the literary criticism. Keble, who probably never read a novel up to this stage in his life and disliked "mere storytelling," was not the best candidate to review Scott, though Keble did describe him as the greatest poet of his generation. Yet the reviewer-critic managed to describe Scott as an Anglo-Catholic writer. This fairly odd description of Scott derived from his writing about the pre-Reformation period of English history and his apparent sympathy with medieval Catholicism. The Waverly novels, in Keble's eyes, were not really novels at all, but poetic romances, forms of the nineteenth-century epic and closely akin to the works of Homer and Virgil.

A more important aspect of Keble's essay is to be found in the rejection of Aristotle's definition of poetry as a form of imitation. According to Keble, poetry was

> ...the indirect expression in words, most appropriately in metrical form, of some over-powering emotion, or ruling taste, or feeling, the direct expression whereof is somehow repressed.[18]

By the time of this essay, Keble had broken completely with some of his earlier Neo-Classicism, but I believe his "Romantic" criti-

---

[18]*British Critic* 24 (October 1838): 423-83; reprinted in Liddon, *Occasional Papers and Reviews,* 1-80, 8.

cism was the result of his own concerns for what literature was/
is, rather than the result of his reading in Wordsworth's poetry
and prose or any of the other Romantic critics. At least there is
no evidence from the letters and correspondence to suggest that
Keble was in any way affected by Romantic literary theory, and
there are so many important areas of dissent from the theories of
his contemporaries that it might be unwise to identify Keble too
freely with, for example, Wordsworth or Shelley. What was especially distinctive about Scott, as opposed to many nineteenth
century poets, was his modest reserve. Scott hid his private
thoughts in the "legend" that he was describing.

The popularly written essays illustrate several basic ideas that
Keble worked upon at greater length in the *Lectures*. Poetry was
the result of some deep emotion that could not be directly revealed without detriment to modesty and reserve. Religious poetry took the entire created world as its subject matter, and great
poetry—that which reflected the deep emotions of the author and
the sense of either the infinite or man's capacity of knowing right
from wrong—was instinctively religious; for such poetry invariably led the thoughtful reader to contemplate the author of the
world itself.

The Lectures on Poetry

The Lectures on Poetry, consist of forty lectures, delivered between 1832 and 1842 and published in 1844 with a "dedication"
to William Wordsworth, who was not mentioned otherwise in the
lectures. The sheer mass of material that Keble covered with apparent ease makes the *Lectures* one of the most impressive critical efforts of the nineteenth century and difficult to analyze on
more than a superficial level. There is scarcely a text from the literature of Classical antiquity (Greece and Rome) that is not discussed in detail, and there are also frequent references to English
poetry, to poets as various as Shakespeare, Spenser, Byron, and
Sir Walter Scott. In keeping with the Oxford tradition, Keble lec-
tured in Latin, and though he complained once that his meaning
could never be exactly translated into English, a translation was
published in 1912.

In the first six lectures, Keble set forth his theory of the origins
and functions of poetry and the distinction between great, or "pri-

mary" poets and "mere versifiers," or "secondary" poets. Lectures seven through forty present an application of the theory to the poets of Greece and Rome, with an occasional reference to English poets—Shakespeare, Spenser, and several of the recently dead Romantics (Keble never mentioned a living poet in his commentary.)—and a very brief commentary on Dante. The final lectures, however, argue a theme that is implicit throughout the two volumes—the close relationship between poetry and religion, whose origin are argued to to be almost identical.

The origins of poetry are connate with the origins of mankind,[19] and the greatest poetry was a response to the perennial longing of mankind for that which could not be found in human existence. Great poetry was a "divinely bestowed gift" for the relief of emotions, which could never be satisfied in this world. Such poetry was not, as a rule, an unguarded outburst of emotion or a protest against the existing state of things, nor was it an autobiographical record of the poet's emotions. Great poetry was the result of some deep longing on the part of the poet with which most of humanity could identify.

A second characteristic of great poetry was that it was always marked by the quality of reserve. The principle device that the poet used to conceal his emotions was the use of certain characters in his work to convey the author's emotions. Thus Virgil hid behind the character of Achilles. Great poetry, whatever device the poet used, was always distinguished by the poet's tendency to conceal his emotions. The function of poetry was not achieved by the poet's expression of his own "inward convictions"; instead,

> The glorious art of Poetry [was] a kind of medicine divinely bestowed upon man: which gives healing relief to secret mental emotion, yet without detriment to modest reserve.[20]

In spite of the Romantic parallels in these comments on the origins of poetry, Keble's insistence on the control that the poet exercised over his emotions makes the casual identification of

---

[19]*Lectures on Poetry,* trans. Edward K. Francis, 2 vols. (Oxford: James Parker, 1912) 59.

[20]Ibid., 22.

Keble's theory and Wordsworth's a bit premature. Rather, Keble's comments on the origins of poetry (or, for that matter, prose) were consistent with the various comments of writers as diverse as Pope, Swift, and Donne on how and why they came to write their works. Emotions in themselves did not make for great poetry, for poetry was always noted for its adherence to form and organization. Poetry was largely the "result of madness" and best enjoyed by those with a "mind full of overflowing," but it was always written in a traditional form and marked by reserve in its depiction of the emotions common to mankind.

Keble was deliberately vague in his discussion of the various emotions that gave rise to poetry and were, in turn, purified by it; but it is quite clear that he did not mean any of the emotions that we would describe as passions. He used the word *catharsis* only once in the whole of the lectures, and it is obvious that he thought the grand emotions were not a vital part of the human experience. "The strong passions," he remarked, "visit us but rarely." In keeping with the infrequency of the more passionate feelings, Keble addressed himself almost exclusively to the "gentler" and more commonly experienced emotions. One of the most characteristic notes in Keble's theory is to be found in his commentary on the kinds of emotions that resulted in poetry and were ultimately satisfied by it. Quoting a passage from Quintillian, he remarked,

> Emotion is of two kinds; the Greeks call the one *pathos*, which we may fittingly render, feeling; the other *ethos*, a word which . . . has no precise equivalent: *mores* we call it, or character. The former they have called passionate feelings, the later mild and gentle: by the one men are vehemently excited, by the other they are calmed: the one overpowers us, the other persuades.[21]

Balaam was the type who exhibited *pathos*, while "Job has bequeathed us the poetic expression of an *ethos,* or saintly character."[22] The difference between the two emotions was vital to Keble's theory in general, for there is almost no discussion of the

---

[21]Ibid., 88.

[22]Ibid.

violent emotions, pity and fear for example, to be found in much dramatic literature. In opposition to one scholar who has suggested that Keble's theory of the function of poetry was to stimulate catharsis in the poet,[23] it should be noted that for Keble it was the gentler and more common emotions that were the substance of great poetry. The best poetry, he remarked, was the product of those emotions that penetrate the whole of the poet's life.

Keble's description of the kind of emotion to which poetry was primarily addressed is elemental in understanding his apparently subjective classification of poets as either secondary or primary. The "fine frenzy" of many of his contemporaries was not the best source of poetry, for such poetry seemed to admit of no form of "law or control" external to itself. The great poets concealed their feelings, and used their characters to speak for themselves. This is one of the very few points of agreement between Keble's and Aristotle's comments on Homer's knowledge of when to speak in his own person and when to conceal himself through assuming the voice of one of his characters.[24] Primary poets, then, were inevitably characterized by the enduring emotions and by the habit of reserve in concealing their own emotions through the use of certain characters to articulate those feelings. Secondary poets were just the opposite. They felt no shame at all in revealing themselves through their work or in pandering to the baser emotions of their audience. Such poets seemed to write for no other purpose than that of drawing attention to themselves. Hence they were always attracted to the paradoxical and novel elements of life.

Such comments anticipate one of the most controversial elements in the *Lectures* as a whole and provide one of the reasons why Keble has found so little favor with modern readers. Keble's thematic insistence that the greatest poets (with the exception of

---

[23]Cf. George B. Tennyson, "The Sacramental Imagination," in *Nature and the Victorian Imagination,* ed. George Tennyson and U. C. Knoepflmacher (Berkeley CA: University of California Press, 1977) 370.

[24]Francis, *Lectures on Poetry,* 1:121.

John Milton) were conservative in their political and religious outlook has drawn the fire of at least one modern critic.

> Keble was genuinely concerned about the state of the poor, yet talk of "honourable poverty" comes uneasily from the official spokesman of the most privileged corporation of the land.[25]

The criticism of the above passage was directed at Keble's praise of Wordsworth's ability to dignify the state of the rural poor in England; but the comments, if true, overturn the *Lectures* completely. Keble really was a conservative and he, rightly or wrongly, believed that the great poets were conservative in their "aristocratic" sympathies and pervasive contempt of reformers. Again and again, he touched on this idea that the primary poets were inevitably on the "aristocratic side" in their praise of the legitimate leaders of society and their condemnation of those who would be regarded as "liberal" in the nineteenth century. The Homeric heroes were obviously a reflection of Homer's personal belief in a structured society; and his condemnation of Penelope's suitors might be taken as the conservative response to liberalism.

> Homer could hardly, at least to my thinking, have more exactly reflected the mind of those who, without hesitation, prefer their own happy condition, however antiquated, however obsolete and old fashioned, to the untried nostrums of reformers. . . . We are not altogether unfamiliar with this sort of generosity on the lips of popular reformers; and have either at some time known, or at all events heard of, men who while violently overriding civil rights, profess their respect for private property with astonishing zeal.[26]

The first volume might be summarized as follows. Poetry was almost a divinely inspired instrument whereby the poet achieved a personal relief from the besetting anxieties of life. These anxieties were of an enduring kind and not, as a rule, the result of the more violent emotions. Poetry was the divinely bestowed instrument through which the poet and his reader achieved a quiet re-

---

[25]Samuel L. Prickett, *Romanticism and Religion* (Cambridge: Cambridge University Press, 1976) 98.

[26]Francis, *Lectures on Poetry*, 1:242.

lief (ethos) in making a poem; and this relief was the basis for the "peculiar charm" of poetry. For this reason, poetry had the power "to appease a yearning desire which for the present is denied satisfication" and was thus a kind of spiritual and intellectual medicine through which the poet gave utterance to his deepest emotions while maintaining a modest reserve in concealing hismself in what he wrote. The best poets were men in the persistent grip of some deep emotion. Through the act of writing, they achieved a gentle (versus cathartic) cleansing of emotions.

The greatest poets were men of the keenest sensibilities, resembling in many ways the insane in their persistent grief that troubled them; and the "madness" of the poet gave to his work its most distinguishing feature. The poet wrote to relieve his feelings, but the end result of his work was an affirmation of an ordered society and the goodness of God. In addition to the deeply felt emotions that were the stimulus of great poets, there were also external proofs by which the poet could be judged. Great poetry was always marked by a quiet reserve on the part of the author and a consistency of attitude. As Aristotle had suggested, Homer always knew when to speak in his own person and when to speak through one of his characters; and this quality was to be found in all the major poets.

The primary poets were also distinguished by other features. As a rule, such poets were invariably conservative in their religious and political beliefs. Each seemed to express a belief in the basic goodness of God and the providential course of human history. Each was known for the consistent ideology of his work and his contempt for the popular fashions of the day.

The best audience for poetry was the young. The pleasures of poetry were so deeply emotional in character that it was almost impossible for anyone but the "enthusiastic" to fully appreciate poetry. Yet one of the great pleasures of poetry could be enjoyed by the mature reader as well, for among the chief pleasures of poetry was its presentation of a moral universe. The best poetry was inevitably addressed to the ethical perceptions of the individual reader, and one of the aspects of the "peculiar charm" of poetry was its appeal to those universal moral laws. Another feature of great poetry was the assistance it provided in the development of an *"ethos,"* or "saintly character," through the poet's efforts to portray a moral universe. The need for a belief in a morally ordered universe and a benevolent God was all the more imperative in such "perilous times" as the early nineteenth century, when all existing institutions appeared to be nearing a state of collapse. Thus poetry was almost the most important form of "recreation" for civilized man.

Keble must have known of the invitation to continue his term as lecturer long before he reached the end of his original five-year term. The invitation to continue as Professor of Poetry is of course a significant comment on the impression that he was making in the course of his original term, and the second set of lectures presents almost no new ideas about poetry and only the fewest number of revisions from his earlier comments. In volume two, however, one will notice an apparent growth in the personal confidence of the lecturer, for there is far less hesitation in the various assertions about individual poets or critics. The second volume pushes some of the ideology of the earlier lectures to its logical extreme, and we find Keble identifying the aims of poetry as identical to those of religion. For it was Nature that prompted the idea of reserve in religion and poetry. Scripture itself suggested the idea:

> ... all who carefully try to imitate Nature are forced to observe a certain restraint and reserve: at least thus far, that, like her, they approach each stage of beauty by a quiet and well-ordered movement. . . . The whole principle of piety, such at least as is wisely governed, is ordered by the rule divinely laid down in Holy Scripture, that things of highest worth should . . . not be offered to listless and unprepared minds; but only brought into the light when the eyes of those who gaze on them have been disciplined and purified. Lastly, both in Poetry and in Religion, an indefinably tender and keen feeling for what is past or out of sight or yet to come, will ever assert and claim a high place of honour for itself. . . . Thus the very practice and cultivation of Poetry will be found to possess, in some sort, a power of guiding and composing the mind to worship and prayer. . . . it follows that whatever is wont to corrupt and undermine Religion will to a great degree correspond with that which injures and degrades poets and poetry.[27]

---

[27]Ibid., 2:462-63.

Given the religious tone of the lectures, it is no surprise that Keble has fallen into such neglect in the present century, but it might be noted that there is very little that might be called "sentimental" in the above or in the lectures as a whole. The comments on the relationship between poetry and religion are closely reasoned, but of course everything depends on a belief in the existence of some higher power.

It should be noted that Keble's own form of Christianity did not prevent him from enjoying a body of work completely alien to his own beliefs. The various "monkeyshines of the Gods" (I. A. Richard's phrase) that beset the heroes of Homer and the Greek dramatists held no peril of belief for Keble, for the activities of the gods invariably reflected the human impulse towards the virtue of justice.[28]

The major poets that are discussed in the second series of lectures include Aeschylus, Pindar, Lucretius, Sophocles, and Euripides, but there are brief comments on several English poets, including Herbert and Southey. Each of these poets illustrates the ideas that Keble had set forth in his first volume. Each practiced, in one way or another, the principle of reserve, often by the use of allegory and sometimes, as in the case of George Herbert, by an apparent trifling with his subject. Each was a conservative in his support of the traditional religious beliefs of his time and in his concern for the illustration of divine justice in his work.

The one apparent exception to all of the above was the extensive commentary of Lucretius's *De Rerum Natura*. In the one doctoral study on Keble's aesthetics, the author complained that Keble was too much involved with the morals and religion of the poet to render an objective judgment on his work. Whatever might be said about Keble's other literary judgments, that analysis certainly does not stand if we examine his several lectures on Lucretius.[29] Lucretius was a primary poet, and his alleged atheism

---

[28]Ibid., 1:6-16.

[29]Ibid., 2:332; John T. Reed, "A Critical Analysis of the Literary Theories of John Keble" (Ph.D. diss., Northwestern University, 1957) 173.

could be explained by noting that he was (according to several of his contemporaries) mentally disturbed. The reader could escape the poet's atheism by attending to other elements in his poem, especially its beautiful language and tone. The reader, as in the case of other "immoral" works of art, could easily turn his attention away from the offensive passages. Having praised Lucretius's achievement, Keble turned his attention to a modern "atheist," Shelley. The Romantic poet was less to be excused than his Roman counterpart for he had the infinite advantage of being exposed to "true religion" and frequently expressed his contempt for that great blessing. Still, Shelley was a poet of the greatest potential and was to be considered as almost a primary poet for the great power of emotion and imagination that he illustrated in his work.

> . . . of utterance, so far as regards this morbid philosophy, even more outrageous and unbridled, but in command of language and of rhythm, an even greater master [than Lucretius], and . . . of far more sensitive temperament. But it was, one fancies with some probability, that even he was scarcely master of himself. In short, they were, and are now, both then, considered rather as unhappy than as impious. This fact should show us how strong is the tendency of human nature on the side of goodness and piety.[30]

The concern for goodness in its many forms, whether something as slight as a beautiful flower or as grand as the scarcely visible system of divine justice, was characteristic of all the great poets, and thus it was that all of the primary poets reflected "the reverence due to the Gods, the hope of immortality, and lastly, the belief that virtue is impressed on us, not by laws alone, but by Nature herself."[31]

Thus all the poetry of classical antiquity was a kind of prophecy of the system that was formally revealed in the New Testament, as the greatest of the Christian poets, Dante, has shown in the high reverence that he paid towards his pagan mentors.

---

[30]Francis, *Lectures on Poetry*, 2:330.

[31]Ibid., 2:464.

Keble concluded his lectures on an almost mystical level with his description of those "essential principles" that poetry and religion have in common. With the aid of Christian theology, everything that had "seemed secular and profane" was illumined "with a new and celestial light." Poetry became the guide "to the very utterances of Nature, or . . . the Author of Nature." With such an inheritance, the poet must be governed by a deep sense of Christian reserve. It was no accident that so many of the poets of the Christian epoch had used allegory to conceal themselves and their message. Even obscurity itself was preferable to the direct promulgation of the sacred truths of Christianity.

The origin of poetry was closely akin to that of prayer, and "the very practice and cultivation of Poetry" would be seen to have the power of directing the mind towards "worship and prayer." Therefore, whatever exerted a corrupting influence on religion— liberalism and the open revelations of the self, for example— tended to corrupt poetry. The nineteenth century's habit of praising the immoral aspects of poetry was, in Keble's judgment, a kind of idolatry. When critics praised poetry without conviction, they were engaging in a lesser form of hypocrisy. For that reason, Keble suggested that the reader of poetry ought to possess the same qualities that were to be found in great literature. It was a matter of *Cor ad cor loquitur*.

Conclusion

By the time Keble had come to the end of his second term as lecturer, the Protestant reaction against the Tractarian program had set in. His intended successor, Isaac Williams, was defeated in the Oxford election because of his tract on reserve ("On Reserve in Communicating Religious Knowledge," Nos. 80, 87), the very idea that Keble had been developing in his lectures. Yet there were other crises during his final years as lecturer that probably had an even more distressing effect on Keble. Newman was known to be moving towards Rome. *The Tracts for the Times* were in disgrace with the bishops, and the question of Erastianism was more prominent than it had ever been. None of these disastrous developments influenced Keble as lecturer, but the outcry against the Oxford Movement might explain the intense piety and apparent escapism of his conclusion. Whatever we might think about Keble's commentary on the kinship of poetry and religion, he was following some excellent sources, including St. Paul, St. Augustine, and a host of medieval Christian poets. Keble was obviously working in the Romantic ethos when he composed his lectures; but his critical affinities were much closer to what is now called "medieval aesthetics" in the sense that all poetry serves "our doctryne." The commentary on the relationship of poetry and religion separates Keble from his Romantic and Victorian contemporaries. For poets as different as Wordsworth, Shelley, and Arnold, poetry was a superior alternative to religion, rather than its handmaiden.

The most striking and original aspect of Keble's *Lectures on Poetry* is not his commentary on the origins and functions of poetry and the pre-Freudian aspects of that commentary. Many poets and writers have openly stated that they wrote their work for the very reason that Keble describes as the basis for great poetry. I believe it is in the commentary on the political and religious conservatism that underlies great poetry that Keble has made his most significant discovery. As we have seen, there has been a reaction on the part of modern scholars against Keble's description of Wordsworth as a conservative, but the description applies at least to Wordsworth's middle and late poems; and the idea that Homer, Virgil, and the Greek dramatic poets were, ultimately, on the side of established institutions is now an accepted theme in modern classical studies.

Chapter III

The Christian Year

The Christian Year was first published anonymously in 1827. A complete edition was published the following year when Keble added a series of poems in honor of certain state "feast days." Most of his friends knew that Keble was the author of the book. Newman remarked briefly, "Keble's hymns are just out . . . they seem quite excellent."[1] As I have earlier remarked, sales of the volume came to be one of the great success stories of the nineteenth century. *The Christian Year* was certainly important to the reader of poetry in the Victorian age.[2] Yet no one wrote about Keble's poetry during his lifetime. It was only with the edition of 1866 (the year of his death) and later that reviewers began to discuss the significance of Keble's volume.

At the time of writing and publishing his first volume, Keble was not yet what might be called an Anglo-Catholic, and it is therefore questionable whether the work can be regarded as a "Tractarian" text. Throughout the poetry we find references to

---

[1]*Letters and Diaries of John Henry Newman,* ed. Gerald Tracey (Oxford: Clarendon Press, 1979) 2:20.

[2]Thomas Mozley, *Reminiscences Chiefly of Oriel College and the Oxford Movement,* 2 vols. (Boston: Houghton Mifflin Co., 1882) 1:219.

"principles" of religion that the Oxford Movement later opposed. Yet there is a link between the poetry and the ideology of 1833, for one of the ideas in *The Christian Year* is that the clergy of the Church of England should reform itself. Indeed, the reform motif of the poetry is one of its most interesting elements.

If Keble's poetry does not readily accommodate itself to the later ideals of "National Apostasy" or the *Tracts for the Times,* it is even more of a mistake to suggest that he was working under the influence of George Herbert or William Wordsworth. Keble denied that Herbert had been an influence on his poetry, and in various places apologized for the "quaint" imagery of his supposed mentor. The influence of Wordsworth is even more suspect if we remember Keble's earlier review of Wordsworth's first two volumes of poetry; but even at a much later date, when he was writing his "Dedication" of the lectures to Wordsworth, he expressed a concern to J. T. Coleridge that he did not wish to seem to give approval to the "pantheistic air" in Wordsworth.[3] Keble's approach to Nature, I will argue, is wholly different from that of his supposed mentor, and the phrase used to describe Keble's approach—"sacramental imagination"—is very different in the uses it makes of the created world.[4]

The Purpose of *The Christian Year*

In his "Advertisement" (actually a brief preface) to the volume, Keble declared that his purpose in writing and publishing *The Christian Year* was to promote a "sober standard of feeling in matters of practical religion" at a time when "excitement of every kind is sought after with a morbid eagerness." He concluded his brief preface by noting that his intention was to recommend the "soothing" tendency of the Anglican Prayer Book.

---

[3]Keble to Coleridge, April 1844, CC.

[4]Cf. George B. Tennyson, "The Sacramental Imagination," in *Nature and the Victorian Imagination,* ed. George B. Tennyson and U. C. Knoepflmacher (Berkeley CA: University of California Press, 1977) 370-75; also, Gerald Tennyson, *Victorian Devotional Poetry: The Tractarian Mode* (Berkeley CA: University of California Press, 1981) 72.

> The object of the present publication will be attained if any per-
> son finds assistance from it in bringing his own thoughts and
> feelings into more entire unison with those recommended and
> exemplified in the Prayer Book. . . . Something has been added
> at the end concerning the several Occasional Services: which
> constitute, from their personal and domestic nature, the most
> perfect instance of the *soothing* tendency in the Prayer Book,
> which it is the chief purpose of these pages to exhibit.

In these brief comments, we can understand why Keble's poetry
has been so generally ignored by twentieth-century readers. The
idea of poetry being used to soothe or quiet the emotions is completely alien to a modern reader's expectations of what poetry, including religious poetry, should do for the reader. Yet it was this
quality that Keble admired most of all in the poetry of Wordsworth, and one of the feelings that Keble sought to promote was
a proper attitude towards poverty.

> I have [he told Wordsworth] many thoughts in my mind of the
> desirableness of engaging all ranks of people more immediately
> in the service of the Church . . . nothing would lead more se-
> curely to such a purpose than enducing them [the poor] to feel
> rightly about poverty.[5]

Such was Wordsworth's great achievement. As Keble wrote in the
dedication to his *Lectures on Poetry,* Wordsworth was a poet who
had described the "manners and religion of the poor . . . in an celestial light." While it is easy to dismiss such a tribute, Keble was
in earnest in his praise of the quieting power of Wordsworth's poetry. The great lesson of the Prayer Book was "cheerful obedience"; Wordsworth, almost alone of the Romantic poets, had
nurtured just that spirit in his descriptions of the country poor.

Yet *The Christian Year* is more than a complacent description
of English rural society and religion. As we will see, the most important link between Keble's poetry and the Oxford Movement of
1833 is its quiet call for a reformation in the lives of the English
rural clergy and in the poetry of his own age.

---

[5]Mary Moorman, *William Wordsworth,* 2 vols. (Oxford: Oxford University Press, 1965) 2:542-43.

The major theme in *The Christian Year* is the love of God for the whole of the created world. That love created in man an obligation to reciprocate, either by a more zealous performance of his duties or a cheerful acceptance of his place in life. Nature is the best example of God's love for mankind, and in Keble's frequent poems about Nature we find a very different approach to his subject from that which is commonly called "Romantic." In Keble's poetry, the beauties and varieties of Nature provide the most striking proof for the existence of God. Keble's argument, so far as it may be called such, derives from Butler's *Analogy of Religion* and personal experience. Nature presented a link between God and Man, and Keble's poetic meditations of Nature always lead the reader upwards to a contemplation of God. The poet's method, however, is seldom direct, for it is the analogy between religion and Nature that Keble finds so instructive.

There are exceptions to this method, and the reader should not be misled by Keble's comments on the "soothing" tendency of either the Prayer Book or his own poetry. Several of the poems are concerned with the low spiritual state of the Anglican clergy and "the ruler of the Christian land"—the king or his representatives. In the poems about the clergy Keble sometimes sounds like a contributor to some of the "liberal" or radical journals of his day, for he witnessed the apparent laziness of his clerical brethren on a firsthand basis. In his frequent poems on poetry, Keble was severe with the egotism and sensuality of his fellow poets.

Yet the reforming motif in Keble's poetry is urged so gently that it does not take away from Keble's ideal as expressed in the Advertisement. Each of the poems sustains the major theme in *The Christian Year*. Keble, as a rule, followed the scriptural text of the service for the day, and the poems might be read as a meditation on the text. Occasionally, the poet did throw off some of his natural restraint, and it was no accident that one of his closest friends warned him of sounding very like a "methodist" in his response to scripture or Nature.[6] Yet Keble was able to balance

---

[6]*Remains of Richard Hurrell Froude,* ed. John Henry Newman and John Keble, 4 vols. (Oxford: James Parker, 1838-1839) 1:232.

his own natural piety and simplicity by constantly appealing to the beauties of creation. As a recent scholar has noted, Nature in the eyes of Keble was the instrument by which we gained our knowledge of God; it was "the handmaiden to divine truth."[7] It should be added that such a view was largely Keble's own and not that of Oxford or the Oxford Movement. Both of Keble's closest friends, Newman and Froude, were unmoved by Keble's proofs for the existence of a benevolent God.

The Poetry

The Christian Year opens with a set of companion poems, "Morning" and "Evening," an idea taken perhaps from the method of Bishop Ken's *Hymns for All the Festivals of the Year,* published after Ken's death in 1721. (Ken was a nonjuring bishop whom Keble referred to frequently in his letters and in several places throughout his sermons.) Both of Keble's poems set the tone for the volume as a whole in that each was to be read as a meditative prayer or hymn. Two lines from "Morning" serve to illustrate what Keble's critics and admirers believe is most attractive or sentimental in the poetry.

> *And help us, this and every day,*
> *To live more nearly as we pray.*

Simple, direct, and possibly banal—the lines and the sentiments conveyed in them are almost too much for a modern reader or critic. Of course, there is nothing startling or original in the idea, but it is the very opposite of "simplistic" or insipid. To follow the mandates of the Lord's Prayer is surely the most challenging task that a Christian can undertake.

The diction of "Morning" has its closest affinities with Neo-Classicism, especially, one might suggest, with the odes of Collins and shorter poetry of Samuel Johnson. And in its emphasis on the basics of the Christian life, the ideology is much closer to the eighteenth century. Keble directly advised against a life of excessive zeal. The Christian life was not to be found in "the cloistered cell".

---

[7]Tennyson, *Victorian Devotional Poetry,* 96.

> *We need not bid, for cloistered cell*
> *Our neighbor and our work farewell,*
> *Nor strive to wind ourselves too high*
> *For sinful man beneath the sky . . .*

Rather, Keble emphasized, the saintly life was to be found in "each returning day," in "the trivial round, the common task," and "in our daily course." The Christian spirit could adorn the most humble aspects of life.

> *Old Friends, old scenes, will lovelier be,*
> *As more of Heaven in each we see:*
> *Some softening glean of love and prayer*
> *Shall dawn on every cross and care.*

"Evening" uses the same verse form and stanzaic pattern, and its message is closely parallel to the above: the love of God can make the most prosaic activity into a religious exercise. But Keble introduced an idea into "Evening" that was one of the major themes in *The Christian Year* —the reform of the lower clergy. Such a theme in itself explicitly challenges the idea that Keble was an establishment man and indifferent to the highly visible problems in the Church of England. Towards the end of the poem, we read,

> *Oh, by Thine own sad burthen borne*
> *So meekly up the hill of scorn,*
> *Teach Thou Thy Priests their daily cross*
> *To bear as Thine, nor count it loss!*

Keble, in the above and in other poems, was encouraging the clergy to look more critically at itself and its performance of priestly duties. The concluding line, " . . . nor count it loss," served as a comment on the social climbing clergy who neglected humbler duties in pursuit of a better living or an episcopal see.

As in the opening poem, Keble argued that the real basis for the Christian life, and the standard by which each of us will be judged, is to be found in the performance of our daily duties.

There is another idea in "Evening" that is important because it marks the religious difference between the poems and the Oxford Movement (1833-1845). The idea was that the king, or his agents (Prime Minister and Parliament), was head of the Church of England.

The Rulers of this Christian land,
'Twixt Thee and us ordained to stand,—
Guide Thou their course, O Lord, aright
Let all do all as in thy sight.

My reading of these lines, placed as they are between the comments on the Anglican clergy, suggests that in 1827 Keble upheld the traditional notion that the king (or his representatives) was the "head" of the English church and people an idea confirmed by Keble's later description of the English monarch as "nursing father" of the church (a metaphor taken from the Old Testament, and the topic of Keble's sermon of 5 November 1835). Based on these lines and the description of the king as a "nursing father" to the church, I would suggest that Keble was an upholder of the Erastianism that he and his colleagues in the Oxford Movement were to later challenge.

In the first poem of the text proper, "The First Sunday after Advent," Keble returned to his comments on the lower clergy in the church. The poem opens,

Awake! again the Gospel-trump is blown

This almost stern note is reiterated in the body of the poem where we find the poet criticizing his colleagues for their lack of faith and charity.

Awake! why linger in the gorgeous town,
Sworn liegemen of the Cross and thorny crown?
Up from your beds of sloth for shame

Following this indictment of the clergy, Keble offered a long commentary on hypocrisy in the national church. Yet the poem is not an indictment of the clergy in the style of Milton. The church has always been a mixture of "the chosen few" and the hypocrites. In all likelihood Keble's poem was based on direct observation and, notwithstanding his complaints about an indolent clergy, the real thrust of the poem is against the political liberals of the day with "the changeful burden still of their rude lawless cry."

There is one more idea in this poem that might be noted. Having surveyed the disastrous episodes—"decaying ages"—of church history, Keble advised his readers to turn aside from the controversies of the moment in favor of waiting patiently for the final moment.

Thus bad and good their several warnings give
Of His approach, whom none may see and live:
    Faith's ear, with awful still delight
    Counts them like minute-bells at night,
Keeping the heart awake till dawn of morn,
While to her funeral pile this aged world is born.

The reforming impulse is throughout *The Christian Year*. For the most part it is directed against the clergy of the Church of England, but on one occasion ("Thursday Before Easter") Keble seems to attack the king.

Oh! grief to think that grapes of gall
    Should cluster round thine healthiest shoot!
God's herald prove a heartless thrall,
    Who, if he dared, would fain be mute!
Even such in this bad world we see. . .

The answer to the widespread corruptions in the government and in the church was not revolution. The lesson of bad clergy was that men should turn away from such problems, ". . . and trembling strive / To keep the lingering flame in thine own heart alive."

There are other themes in Keble's first volume that might be noted, for they also are quite peculiar to either the Church of England or Keble's ancestral background. The most striking of these is the recurrent praise of virginity as the highest state of the Christian life. In several poems Keble praised in an extraordinary way Mary, as the Virgin Mother of God, the supreme object of veneration in the Christian life. In the poem "Wednesday Before Easter" the praise of virginity is amplified to be slightly lower than that of martyrdom in the kingdom of God. I quote from the fourth and following stanzas:

They say, who know the life divine,
And upward gaze with eagle eyne,
That by each golden crown on high,
Rich with celestial jewelry
Which for our Lord's redeemed is set,
There hangs a radiant coronet,
All gemmed with pure and living light,
Too dazzling for a sinner's sight,
Prepared for virgin souls, and they

Who seek the Martyr's diadem.
Nor deem, who to that bliss aspire,
Must win their way through blood and fire.
The writhings of a wounded heart
Are fiercer than a foeman's dart.
Oft in Life stillest shade reclining,
In Desolation unrepining,
Without a hope on earth to find
A mirror in an answering mind,
Meek souls there are, who little dream
Their daily strife an Angel's theme,
Or that the rod they take so calm

*   *   *   *   *   *

Shall prove in Heaven a martyr's palm.
By purest pleasures unbeguiled
To idolise a wife or child;
Such wedded souls our God shall own
For faultless virgins round his throne.

The ideal of celebate priesthood was later posited during the Oxford Movement as one of the remedies for a lethargic, caste-conscious clergy—"pampered aristocrats," as Froude later put it—but the ideal survived only in the person of Newman.

Another important subject in *The Christian Year* was the state of poetry in the early nineteenth century. It is fairly obvious that Keble was unhappy with the work of most nineteenth-century poets. He may have been referring only to Byron and the "miserable school" of Mr. Leigh Hunt, but the indictment of Romantic poets sounds much more comprehensive.

In several of his poems Keble commented on what he thought was the essential task of a poet living in a Christian society. "Palm Sunday" is a fair example of Keble's theory. The poem resembles Gray's "Progress of Poesy" with its mixture of Hebrew and Greek influences, but Gray's poem of course celebrates the rise of poetry, while Keble's was an extended lament over the decline of poetry in his own time. Both poets were heavily indebted to the *Psalms* of David. Keble's argument, in part, was that the God who inspired David should inspire the modern poet. Both poets regarded poetry as a kind of sacred rite, yet Keble's comments on poetry transcend two ideas in Gray's "Progress." All that was necessary for the inspiration of the Christian poet was scripture and Nature.

The epigraph to the poem, "If these should hold their peace, the stones would immediately cry out," (Luke 19: 40) provides a clue to Keble's meaning and method. The relevant stanzas are:

> Ye whose hearts are beating high
> With the pulse of Poesy,
> Heirs of more than royal race,
> Framed by Heaven's peculiar grace,
> God's own work to do on earth,
> (If the word be not too bold,)
> Giving virtue a new birth,
> And a life that ne'er grows old—
>
> Sovereign masters of all hearts!
> Know ye, Who hath set your parts?
> He who gave you breath to sing,
> By whose strength ye sweep the string,
> He hath chosen you, to lead
> His Hosannas here below;—
> Mount, and claim your glorious meed;
> Linger not with sin and woe.
>
> Then waken into sound divine
> The very pavement of Thy shrine
> Till we, like Heaven's star-sprinkled floor,
> Faintly give back what we adore
> Childlike though the voices be,
> And untunable the parts,
> Thou wilt own the minstrelsy,
> If it flow from childlike hearts.

The poet was like a priest who was failing to perform his sacred task. The phrase, "Heaven's peculiar grace," suggests that Keble had come to accept the Romantic premise that the poet was different from the rest of humanity. Yet in Keble's insistence that the mission of the poet was religious we find a significant distance that separates him from most Romantic poets. In the comments, "Linger not with sin and woe," Keble expressed his concern for the subject matter of so many of his contemporaries, particularly the work of Lord Byron.

In another poem Keble raised the topic of the proper material for the poet in a Christian society. "The Fourth Sunday after Trinity" proposes the idea that all poems about Nature are religious poems. In a series of quatrains he celebrates the poetic impulse and its finest expression—the praise of God and the world that God created.

> *It was not then a poet's dream,*
> *An idle vaunt of song,*
> *Such as beneath the moon's soft gleam*
> *On vacant fancies throng;*
>
> *Which bids us see in heaven and earth,*
> *In all fair things around,*
> *Strong yearnings for a blest new birth*
> *With sinless glories crown'd;*
>
> *Which bids us hear, at each sweet pause,*
> *From care and want and toil,*
> *When dewy eve her curtain draws*
> *Over the day's turmoil;*
>
> *In the low chant of wakeful birds,*
> *In the deep weltering flood,*
> *In the whispering leaves,*
> *these solemn words—*
> *"God made us all for good."*

Keble's argument in brief was that Nature and the positive aspects of life were the essential materials for the poet. The theme of these poems, especially those on Nature, imply a criticism of nineteenth-century poets who concerned themselves with the darker aspects of Nature and life itself.

A final example of Keble's theory of poetry is "The Sixth Sunday after Trinity," a poem about the repentance of David. Poetry was almost an instrument of grace for the poet because it inspired love and hope in the reader who might, being so inspired, pray for the poet.

> *If ever, floating from faint earthly lyre,*
> *Was wafted to your soul one high desire,*
> > *By all the trembling hope ye feel,*
> > *Think on the minstrel as ye kneel.*

The grace of contrition, in keeping with Keble's general appeal to the analogies of Nature, is likened to a "silent April rain," and the poetry of David was, in part, a means of his conversion.

The poems about Nature and the analogies of Nature to grace are throughout the whole of *The Christian Year,* but "Septuagesima Sunday" is a convenient starting point, in spite of its "piety." The theme of the poem is illustrated in its scriptural epigraph:

> *The invisible things of Him from the creation*
> *of the world are clearly seen, being understood*
> *of things that are made.* (Romans 1:20)

The poem has been described as Wordsworthian in its style, but its method is rather different. The opening stanzas emphasize Keble's theme.

> *There is a book, who runs may read,*
> *Which heavenly truth imparts.*
> *And all the lore its scholars need,*
> *Pure eyes and Christian hearts.*
>
> *The works of God above, below,*
> *   Within us and around,*
> *Are pages in that book, to show*
> *   How God Himself is found.*
>
> *The glorious sky embracing all,*
> *Is like the Maker's love,*
> *Wherewith encompass'd, great and small,*
> *In peace and order move.*
>
> *The Moon above, the Church below,*
> *A wondrous race they run,*
> *But all their radiance, all their glow,*
> *Each borrows of its Sun.*

In addition to the epigraph, which provides the theological basis for the poem, the use of the material of Nature suggests to me an essential difference from Wordsworth. All of created Nature—its beauties and its terrors—were analogues of God's power and mercy.

Keble's method was to approach God through the evidences of Nature with what he described as the "eye of faith," which enabled man to trace, in spite of human frailties, the hand of God. Keble seemed to urge that it was only through such a process that we could come to know God, Nature, and, by implication, true poetry. It was this method that enabled Keble to find out all that he wished to know about God in even the most prosaic subject matter.

From a naturalistic point of view Keble's approach or method might seem to be unsatisfactory. For Keble Nature, while beautiful in itself, is never viewed alone. Its function is to serve as a stepping stone to something higher.

Such an approach to God and Nature is not without its weaknesses. Keble was not what we would call an optimist about the human condition or even Nature itself, but the reader does get the impression that Keble was somewhat diffident about the painful episodes of the Christian life, in particular the crucifixion. The poems on the subject of Passion Week are among the least satisfying in the *The Christian Year*.

At the same time, however, I cannot deny the impression that Keble's shyness or reserve, from a religious point of view, is sometimes preferable to the direct approach of the Metaphysical poets of the seventeenth century. Dr. Johnson was far from being the only critic to complain of the ease and familiarity with God that the metaphysicals sometimes exhibit. The reader may not always think on the religious subject that was, ostensibly at least, the reason for the poem.

It would be wrong to assume that Keble's faith was complacent, as opposed to the complexities of belief in other religious poets. Several of the poems in the collection exhibit the dark side of human consciousness—the possibility that there may be no God and that faith is no more than a delusion.

"The Sixth Sunday after Epiphany" is one of the most perfect in *The Christian Year* to exhibit this problem. The poem presents no grave problems of interpretation, and a careful reader might trace out the influence of this poem on two more celebrated poets, Matthew Arnold ("Dover Beach") and Emily Dickinson ("Success is Counted Sweetest"). The poem addresses those who wished for an absolute knowledge of God or the knowledge that God does not exist. The middle state of obscure knowledge, "doubt's galling chain," was more oppressive than even a complete negation of God's existence.

Keble was sympathetic to the question and his poem provides his own method of answering that question.

> There are, who darkling and alone,
> Would wish the weary night were gone,
> Though dawning morn should only show
> The secret of their unknown woe:
>
> Who pray for sharpest throbs of pain
> To ease them of doubt's galling chain:
> Only disperse the cloud, they cry,
> And if our fate be death, give light and let us die.
>
> Unwise I deem them. Lord, unmeet
> To profit by Thy chastenings sweet,
> For Thou wouldst have us linger still
> Upon the verge of good or ill,
>
> That on Thy guiding hand unseen
> Our undivided hearts may lean,
> And this our frail and foundering bark
> Glides in the narrow wake of Thy beloved Ark.

Keble argues that the lack of direct evidence for the existence of God is not itself a mystery. Man knows of the existence of God through the exercise of conscience, "Thy guiding hand unseen." That the evidence of God's existence is so frail to "gross mortal" eyes (as he wrote in "Baptism") makes faith a much greater possession. The Christian holds to his "dim" and limited vision through the power of love. Such a vision is worth more than empirical proof, which does not require love or faith.

The scarcity of doctrinal ideas in *The Christian Year* is one of the most significant clues to the work's popularity in the Victorian Age. Doctrine was the religious equivalent of a quality that Keble disliked in poetry—"metaphysics"; and we find him closely following his own precepts in his poetry. General readers did not read poetry for direct instruction in either religion or philosophy. The most notable exception to this rule is Keble's lovely poem on baptism, for the poem anticipates Keble's later activity on behalf of the Catholic principles of Anglicanism. A few of the relevant stanzas are:

> Where is it, mothers learn their love?—
> In every Church a fountain springs

O'er which th' eternal Dove
Hovers on softest wings.

What sparkles in that lucid flood
Is water, by gross mortals eyed;
But seen by Faith, 'tis blood
Out of a dear Friend's side

A few calm words of faith and prayer,
A few bright drops of holy dew,
Shall work a wonder there
Earth's charmers never knew

So far as I have been able to discern, the doctrine of Baptismal Regeneration as suggested in the above is the only Catholic doctrine in the whole of *The Christian Year.* His version of the Eucharist was not.

There are several poems in *The Christian Year* that celebrate the Eucharistic service. None of these suggest a belief in the Real Presence; and in "Gunpowder Treason," (one of the state feast-day poems), Keble offered a version of the Eucharist that seemed to deny such a belief. The critical lines occur towards the end of the poem:

O come to our Communion Feast:
There present in the heart,
Not in the hands, th'eternal Priest
Will His true self impart.

The controversy in the poem centers on Keble's apparent denial of the Real Presence in the above stanza. Keble's biographers and historians of the Oxford Movement have insisted that Keble really meant "Not only in the hands" instead of the apparent denial contained in the original.

In the first edition of *The Christian Year,* which was published after Keble's death in 1866, the lines were changed to read "as in the hands." A controversy greeted the changed version. In the *Quarterly Review,* the Bishop of Oxford (Samuel Wilberforce) published an essay on the poetry in which he denounced the change, while the *Guardian,* an Anglo-Catholic weekly, defended it. The question remains as to who made the change. The accepted version is that Keble approved of it on his deathbed, but there is no record of any significance to justify that explanation.

The rest of the poem is filled with other forms of anti-Catholic statements. It therefore seems unlikely that Keble would have accepted anything like a "high position" on the Eucharist at that stage in his life. Even in his later years Keble was strong in his condemnation of Roman doctrines, including the Real Presence, and his readers were content with the idea that the Eucharistic ritual was only commemorative. Newman did not believe in the doctrine of the Real Presence until his conversion, and then only because the church taught such a doctrine. Further, he was severe in his criticisms of Pusey and the other Anglo-Catholics for their promoting of the doctrine since they violated the Anglican consensus on the subject.[8] It would have been most unlikely that Keble had come up with anything approaching a Catholic teaching on the subject of the Eucharist since he was prone to criticize the eucharistic views of one of his friends for his tendency to "turn good young Protestants into Papists."[9]

Pusey tried to defend the revised version of the lines in a letter to Newman.

> What do you think was the original meaning of the Not in the hands. Do you think that it was really written under the influence of Hooker? . . . Dear J. K's leaving it for so many years is more accountable, if he always understood in the sense of I will have mercy and not sacrifice as he did in later years.[10]

Newman answered Pusey's letter:

> Certainly I have always thought dear Keble meant that verse in an anti-catholic sense, when he wrote it. First, the *draft* of that poem shows it—Next, Hurrell Froude always thought so, and expressly attacks Keble for it in one of the Letters in his Remains. Thirdly, Hooker, though tolerant of the Catholic view does surely himself take the Calvinistic; and Keble was especially a disciple

---

[8]John Henry Newman, *Difficulties Felt by Anglicans,* 2 vols. (Westminster MD: Christian Classics, ed. 1969) vol. 1, ch. 4.

[9]Keble to Arthur Perceval, June 1832, Keble-Perceval Correspondence, Pusey House, Oxford.

[10]*Letters and Diaries of John Henry Newman,* ed. Charles Dessain, (Oxford: Oxford University Press, 1973) 23:43.

of Hooker. According to my own idea, it was Jewel . . . whose writings first opened Keble's eyes to the unsatisfactory doctrine of the Reformers as such, in contradistinction to the high Anglican school; and from that time Keble took a much higher line of theology. . . . [11]

Froude (a younger pupil of John Keble and one of the first members of the Oxford Movement) had complained bitterly about the "Protestantism" of the stanza,[12] but Keble had not responded to the criticism and had left the lines unchanged. He was apparently content with the obvious meaning of the lines and the poem as a whole until some period beyond 1854. There are many other reasons to suggest that Keble was content with the literal meaning of the early editions. The later correspondence with John Taylor Coleridge is filled with references to *The Christian Year*— certain lines, words, the copyrights, illustrations, and so forth— but there is no mention of these lines or any change. If Keble were unhappy with the stanza or with the poem as a whole, he did not tell Coleridge.[13]

However, what Keble did mention about the poetry in his letters to Coleridge is interesting and perhaps relevant to this discussion. Pusey, it appears, had twice offered Keble a thousand pounds for the copyright to the volume; Keble had remarked that he did not trust Pusey on this matter.[14]

It would not be a complete surprise, therefore, if Pusey had obtained the copyright through some agreement with Parker (Keble's publisher) and made the change to suit himself and what he believed would have suited Keble. The letter to Newman, cited above, seems to seek approval for the changed version. Moreover, Pusey's silence, when the controversy was going on in the press

---

[11]Ibid., 43-44.

[12]*Remains of Richard Hurrell Froude,* 1:403.

[13]For example, Keble wrote to James Parker in 1847 to express his satisfaction with the latest edition of *The Christian Year:* "I am *extremely well satisfied* with the style of the book." Keble to James Parker, 28 October 1847, in Lewis Collection, Yale University.

[14]Keble to Coleridge, 19 June 1854, CC.

is striking if we remember that Pusey's method was usually just the opposite: his published letters to the Anglo-Catholic and secular press would easily fill a volume.

The suggestion that Keble approved of the change on his deathbed comes from Dr. Pusey, who did profess a belief in the Real Presence (though never in the Roman sense of the word). In 1879 Pusey wrote and published a small "letter" (actually a pamphlet) to H. P. Liddon on the subject of the revised version. In his letter Pusey admitted that the idea for the changed lines was originally his own.

> I remember saying strongly, "Explanations are useless: they have been made over and over again, and are ignored." [Then, Keble wrote to Liddon] "I have made up my mind, that it will be best when a reprint is called for, to adopt E. B. P's emendation and note with a few words pointing out that it does but express the true meaning of the printed text." The line then, after all, is neither yours nor mine [i.e., neither Pusey's nor Liddon's but Keble's].[15]

Following this, an extract from the *Journal of the Rev. Thomas Keble* (Keble's younger brother) is cited, in which Pusey is told by Thomas Keble's wife to make the change right away.

I have never heard of the journal mentioned by Pusey, and there is reason to suggest that the changed lines and the defense of the change is pretty much of an invention. One of the later Tractarians, who did profess a belief in the principle of the Real Presence (G. A. Denison) and whose interpretation of the Eucharist was rejected by the Privy Council in 1854, noted a difference between himself and Keble on this subject.[16] Certainly the other poetry in *The Christian Year* derives from a generally Protestant view of the English church and its teachings.

---

[15]*Postscript on the Alteration of a Line in* The Christian Year (Oxford: James Parker, 1878) 2; see also Liddon Diaries, 5 September 1856: "A great deal of conversation with Keble. He told me that he had frequently wished to withdraw the words 'Not in the hand but in the heart': but that his friends had prevented him." Liddon House, London.

[16]George A. Denison, *Notes of My Life* (London: Macmillan, 1878) 254.

Quite apart from the many questions about Keble's personal faith or his relationship to either the Neo-Classic or Romantic theory of literature, there is a larger context in which *The Christian Year* ought to be read. The poems, taken as a whole, represent one of the last major, or "widely-read," expressions of a philosophic and religious system once known as "cosmic toryism." This system has been interpreted as a form of complacent conservatism for its resistance to change in the political and social spheres. Keble was deeply embued with that kind of conservatism, but it was not primarily a matter of "looking out for number one." He was a conservative in the sense that St. Paul was a conservative: the established order was the best instrument for promoting the common good.

A second aspect of this "philosophy" is to be found in the domain of mysticism, and it is ultimately beyond human description. It predicates a belief that all human enterprises, including evil itself, tend towards a final good; and it includes an "extinction of one's separate individuality" and "an acceptance of all existence as a part of the divine pattern."[17] The alleged simplicity of *The Christian Year* is most certainly scriptural in its essential premise that, in spite of evil and the general decay of the world, there is a provident God who rules the world.

There is scarcely an item in this system that has not been challenged in our own time. Even in the latter half of the nineteenth century, the various forms of "cosmic toryism" were rejected in favor of an often extreme form of pessimism. It is no accident, as one scholar has pointed out, that three of the major Victorian poems are apocalyptic. In each instance the validity of the Christian promise is directly questioned.[18]

The enduring popularity of Keble's first volume is especially significant, for it represents a continuous reminder that, with all of the many evils of the nineteenth century, there were still rea-

---

[17]Basil Willey, *Eighteenth-Century Background: Studies on the Idea of Nature in Thought of the Period* (Boston: Beacon Press, 1961) 43.

[18]John Rosenberg, *The Fall of Camelot* (Cambridge: Harvard University Press, 1973) 36.

sons for hope. Such a "solution" must always appear complacent. Even so great a man as Cardinal Newman remarked that the *data* of human experience tended to deny rather than confirm the existence of God. Yet Newman would have been the first to insist that the theological virtue of hope was also a Christian duty. It is the virtue of hope that is written so large in Keble's poetry.

Every reader must decide for himself about the merits of *The Christian Year;* but the relevance of Keble's poetry to our own time is especially intense if we remember that many theologians and writers have insisted that the one virtue so lacking in modern man is hope.

Conclusion

In this chapter I have suggested a series of reasons why Keble's first volume is at once good and important. The value of the poems, as in the case of all poetry, is the most difficult part of my argument. The very merits of clarity and simplicity would tend to cause a modern reader to be suspicious, if not contemptuous, of their content. *The Christian Year* was based on a system of belief not so far removed from our time as to attract the antiquarian; but it is based on one that is clearly dated in its essential optimism. It would require a major revolution in theology and philosophy to bring back that belief in a providential Creator who controlled the world and punished evil. For this reason, future students of nineteenth century poetry may find Keble to be the most complex and strange of the Victorian poets.

What might be noted, however, is that Keble was almost a "pure" original in his composition of *The Christian Year.* His limited borrowings were based on a desire to complement those from whom he had learned; but he was always independent and, while such a remark tends to turn us away from the idea that he was a saint, it might help us appreciate the poetry more. *The Christian Year* was not a high-church collection of hymns. It was a collection of the most elevated sentiments belonging to the common experience of Christians.

Chapter IV

Keble and the Oxford Movement

Keble's role in the original Oxford Movement of 1833 to 1845 has been debated since the appearance of Newman's *Apologia,* in which we find Keble described as its "true and primary author," and his sermon, "National Apostasy," its formal beginning.[1] Modern scholars have attacked the accuracy of the Newman comments, saying that the remarks on "National Apostasy" were the result of a kind of nostalgia that Newman felt for the man. Others, looking at Keble's personal shyness have urged that he was not the man to have founded or led any kind of movement.[2] The Newman comments became the "myth of July 14, 1833"[3] and, whatever their motivation, the remarks were wrong. Not even Keble knew that he was doing anything important when he de-

[1]John Henry Newman, *Apologia Pro Vita Sua,* ed. Wilfred Ward (London: Everyman Books, 1912) 42.

[2]Owen Chadwick, ed., *The Mind of the Oxford Movement* (Stanford CA: Stanford University Press, 1960) 30-32.

[3]Frank Cross, *John Henry Newman* (London: Philip Alan, 1933) 162.

livered that fairly routine protest against Whig aggression towards the church.[4]

Keble's closest friend and his first biographer, John Taylor Coleridge, has not helped us in our understanding of Keble's ideology in 1833 or the significance of "National Apostasy," for he barely mentioned the sermon in his brief comments on this vital stage of Keble's life.

> We have long as a Nation passed by Keble's principles in these matters, and I am not about to uselessly re-agitate them, but I have made this particular mention of the Sermon, because out of the same feeling . . . arose that concerted and systematic course of action of which the first fruits were the celebrated Tracts.[5]

As brief as these comments are, they contradict a great deal of what has been written about the Oxford Movement. The comments on "Keble's principles" and Coleridge's reluctance to "uselessly re-agitate them" suggest that Keble, for a brief while at least, was uttering sentiments of his own and not those of either the government or the church. Coleridge's second comment also seems to suggest that in 1868 (the date of his *Memoir*) the principles were dead. Finally, Coleridge's identification of the sermon with the *Tracts for the Times* adds to the notion that perhaps the sermon was an important illustration of ideas that were written out more fully in the *Tracts*. Anglican scholars, ignoring the Coleridge commentary, have argued that there was nothing new in the doctrines of 1833 and that the idea of Keble teaching principles of his own, versus those of the church, is completely false. Keble's greatest boast was that he taught only what he had learned from his father, whose roots went back to the seventeenth-century Anglo-Catholic divines.[6]

---

[4]Georgina Battiscombe, *John Keble: A Study in Limitations* (New York: Alfred A. Knopf, 1964) 152.

[5]John Taylor Coleridge, *A Memoir of the Rev. John Keble,* (Oxford: James Parker, 1868) 211.

[6]Frank Cross, *The Oxford Movement and the Seventeenth Century* (London: S. P. C. K., 1933) 1-10.

As the recipient of many of Keble's most revealing letters, Coleridge knew that Keble in 1833 was very far from the conservative politics of his church and that "National Apostasy" represented a severe break with Keble's ancestral Protestantism, religious liberalism, and Toryism. Keble, in fact, was advocating, a policy for the church that was directly counter to the traditions of his church and family. He was arguing (in an oblique way) for a complete separation of church and state. By his sermon and because of his personal professions of radicalism, he had impressed his two younger friends, Froude and Newman, with a solution to the crisis of a doctrinally indifferent state appointing bishops to the "apostolic church in these realms."[7] From Keble's sermon and its ideal of the church's passive acceptance of efforts of the state to effect a separation of church and state came the original idea of the Oxford Movement: the powers would be separated by a refusal of the bishops to oppose efforts by the Whigs to effect such a gesture.

Keble's position in 1833 is best illustrated by a letter sent to Newman shortly after "National Apostasy" was published.

> I think my mind is made us thus far, that I cannot take the *Oath of Supremacy* in the sense which the Legislature clearly now puts upon it. I cannot accept any curacy or office in the Church of England: but I have not made up my mind that I am bound to resign what I have. . . . I think we ought to be prepared to sacrifice any or all of our endowments sooner than sanction it the [anti-church principle] "take every pound, shilling, and penny, only let us make our own laws."[8]

In the above letter, Keble noted that while he would not accept any living from the existing Church of England, he did not think it necessary to give up what he already possessed since he had given "public notice" (i.e., "National Apostasy") of his position.

---

[7]"National Apostasy," ed. Eugene Fairweather, in *The Oxford Movement* (Oxford: Oxford University Press, 1964) 46.

[8]*Letters and Correspondence of John Henry Newman,* ed. Anne Mozley, 2 vols. (London: Longman's, Green & Co., 1892) 1:484; see also, John Griffin, "John Keble: Radical," *Anglican Theological Review* 53 (July 1971): 164-71.

Still, Keble hoped that such extreme measures as clerical poverty would not result from his sermon and its implications. He preferred the "easier price."

Newman finally believed that Keble was in earnest about his program and was "willing to go lengths." He told Froude that the apostolical party must have a leader and that Keble was probably the best that could be found.[9]

As Keble knew when he delivered his sermon, separation from the state meant a loss of clerical privilege and revenues, but unlike Newman and Froude, he was never really attracted to the idea of poverty or a loss of status among the lower clergy. When the offer of Hursley was presented to him by Sir William Heathcote, he turned his back on the radical ideology of 1833 without a whimper or backward glance.

Keble came to the radicalism of 1833 over the course of several years. In early 1827 he was questioning the rights of the state to interfere in purely spiritual matters of the church, and by 1831 he was even more critical of church-state alliance. In that year he expressed a concern that the alliance would be broken without a word of protest from Oxford, but no one could have guessed the position he would shortly adopt. In a sermon of 1831, Keble still maintained the official conservative line. The alliance was ordained by God, and those who questioned it were agents of the lower powers. Attacking every form of political liberalism in that sermon, he was especially critical of those who expressed any sympathy towards "rebellion." Moreover, at the end of the sermon, Keble gave himself his own *imprimatur,* noting that he was recording a protest in the name of the Church of England.[10]

By the time Keble was invited to deliver the sermon at Oxford in 1833, he had changed his mind on one of the basic ideas of the earlier sermon. In that earlier effort he had invoked St. Paul's

[9]Newman to Richard Hurrell Froude, 10 August 1833, in Newman: Correspondence Public, 2 vols., Birmingham Oratory, Birmingham, England; hereafter, CP.

[10]*Sermons, Occasional and Academical* (Oxford: James Parker, 1847) 130.

mandate on civil obedience against the laity and the state. He contended that both powers should practice the "cheerful obedience" of the Prayer Book. Within an interval of two years Keble had come to believe that the ideal of obedience should be practiced first by churchmen. The church should not resist the claims of the state to its property or revenues or to casting off the church altogether. Such a process was infinitely better than depending on the state and bearing the stigma that the national church was no more than a branch of government. Three days before he delivered "National Apostasy," he wrote to a friend.

> I shall be speaking the thoughts of a very large body of the Clergy of England: who feeling daily that it becomes more and more questionable in point of duty and impossible in point of fact, that we should continue in the same relation we are in at present to the government of the country, are naturally looking round on all fragments of the Church Apostolic. . . . all church-men who are not Erastians (I trust a very considerable party) [will separate from the state], the schismatical body, remaining at such cost, in union with the State.[11]

The above letter is vital to an understanding of the basic ideology of the Oxford Movement. Every churchman who was not an Erastian would separate from the state. Only the Erastians or conservatives would remain "at such cost" with an infidel government.

There is more evidence to suggest that Keble envisioned a reform program far more innovative than scholars have suggested. In a letter of August 1833, Keble described the prospect of spoliation as "wholesome"[12] in its ability to wean churchmen away from a hope of any political settlement with the state. And when the Hadleigh meetings (Hadleigh was the parish of one of the tentative members of the apostolical party—H. Rose) were concluded, Froude wrote to another prospective member of Keble's advanced position in the Tractarian program. One of the basic

---

[11]Keble to Mrs. Pruen, July 1833, in Keble Collection, Keble College, Oxford; hereafter KC.

[12]Keble to Newman, August 1833, CP.

points of Froude's letter was that Keble was unwilling to even protest against the idea of a complete separation from the state: "Keble," said Froude, "demurs to this because he thinks the Union of Church and State . . . actually sinful."[13]

From these letters and the sermon, I believe it can be argued that Keble was indeed the "true and primary author" of the religious revival of 1833. Still, a candid reader might inquire how such an enterprise could be fairly described as "religious." It would seem that the emphasis thus far has been on politics, and it was Keble who set the policy of having "no concern with politics," which would probably hasten the process of disestablishment. Yet there is a second element of anti-Erastianism in such a process. According to each of the first apostolicals, Erastianism and Catholicism were contradictory and mutually exclusive terms for a mode of church governance. Every invocation of the bishop's authority or the ministerial "gift" of the clergy was an indirect hit at the idea that the church belonged to the state.

"National Apostasy"

"National Apostasy" is perhaps the most famous sermon in the history of English ecclesiastical writing; and while it is not as interesting to read as any of Newman's, it is, nevertheless, a perfect expression of the basic ethos of the Oxford Movement. Scholars, who have read the sermon as a Tory protest against the threat of disestablishment and praised Keble for his courage in addressing such strong words in the presence of government officials, have concentrated on the opening half of "National Apostasy"[14] where Keble did indeed upbraid the government for its willingness to tamper with the almost "sacred friendship" between the two powers.

The message of "National Apostasy" comes in its second half. Keble used the Old Testament prophet Samuel and his struggle with Saul as a metaphor for what was happening in the nineteenth-century church. Saul wished to break away from Samuel,

---

[13]Richard H. Froude to Arthur Perceval, 11 August 1833, KC.

[14]Wilhelm J. Beek, *John Keble's Literary and Religious Contributions to the Oxford Movement* (Nijimegen: Centrale Drukkerig, 1959) 28.

and while the prophet believed that the separation of the people from religion is wrong, he gave in to Saul's request. He protested against the immorality of Saul's gesture in alienating the people from their rightful leader, but he gave in and "let the people have their own way." The bishops, Keble advised, should follow the example of Samuel and, while protesting against the immorality of the state's withdrawal from the governance of the church, give in and allow the two powers to be separated.

The lower clergy ought to abandon any hope for a political solution; they should give up all forms of political agitation and concentrate rather on their immediate duties "of piety, purity, charity, justice."[15] And in spite of the pious appearance of Keble's advice to the clergy, the advice was exactly what was needed by most of his colleagues. Such a dedication to the people, if practiced by most of the clergy, would go a long way towards restoring the popular support of the church.

Keble's idea that the lower clergy should give up any efforts towards appeasing the state was a radical solution to both the problem of Erastianism and the quiet worldliness of the Anglican clergy.[16] Keble rightly expected that the first resistance to the Oxford Movement's radical platform would come from the conservatives at Oxford, and the party's title "apostolical" was taken to distinguish their group from the clerical conservatives, "The Friends of the Church." One of Keble's influences on the original revival was a gentler attitude towards the conservatives. Froude habitually referred to them as "Z's," the apostolic term for conservative-Erastian clergy, but through Keble's influence, the relationship was not broken until 1838 when Froude's private comments on the "smug parsons" and "pampered aristocrats" — the "Z's"—became public property.[17]

---

[15]Fairweather, "National Apostasy," 44-47.

[16]John Griffin, "The Meaning of 'National Apostasy': A Note on Newman's *Apologia*," *Faith and Reason* 2 (June 1976): 17-34.

[17]*Remains of Richard Hurrell Froude,* ed. John Henry Newman and John Keble, 4 vols. (Oxford: James Parker, 1838-1839) 1:329.

Keble's influence on the original Oxford Movement, then, was very different from what scholars have assumed. He was no more learned in Anglo-Catholic traditions than any of his friends, and much less the "pastoral" leader of the revival. Rather, he was just what Newman described: the man who gave the first public utterance of a radical platform for securing a complete independence "of the apostolic church in these realms." The church would triumph not through any political assistance, but through its own internal efforts and spirituality.

It is unfortunate that Keble did not follow his own mandates. In 1835 he accepted a clerical appointment (a living) from Sir William Heathcote and settled in to the comfortable life of most of his contemporaries. At a much later time he told another Anglican friend that he considered the Oxford Movement as no more than a "parenthesis" in his life.

> About a year ago, when staying at Hursley, I remember John Keble saying, "I look upon my time with Newman and Pusey as a sort of parenthesis in my life; and I have now returned again to my old views such as I had before. At the time of the great Oxford Movement, when I used to go up to you at Oxford, Pusey and Newman were full of the wonderful progress and success of the Movement—whereas I had always been taught that the truth *must* be unpopular and despised, and to make confession for it was all that one could do."[18]

Somewhat unfairly, Keble told Williams that he had been "carried off my legs" by the excitement of Pusey and Newman over the revival's original success.[19] In later years he apparently told other friends that he had been Newman's unwilling "tool."[20]

It should be noted that either Keble was not telling the truth to Isaac Williams or that his memory failed him. As Williams remarked in his *Autobiography,* Pusey had been very suspicious of

---

[18]*The Autobiography of Isaac Williams,* ed. George Prevost (London: Longman's, Green & Co., 1892) 118.

[19]Ibid., 118.

[20]Charles Dessain, ed., *Letters and Diaries of John Henry Newman,* 28:353.

the early Oxford Movement's ideals and had deliberately signed his name to his first contribution the *Tracts for the Times* to avoid identification with others in the revival.[21] Keble, moreover, was the author of many of the most radical letters in the "apostolical" circle. Keble's remark that the "truth *must* be unpopular" also contradicts many of his statements and writings of 1833, when he remarked that many would take up the apostolic program in their resistance to state control of the church. At the same time, the remarks are valuable because they confirm one of the major themes in this study—that Keble changed his mind about many important ideas, including the religious revival of 1833.

Thus, Keble's vicarage at Hursley was not the first Tractarian parish. A good living in the countryside was one of the greatest temptations that the Establishment could offer its clergy. This was in sharp contrast to the apostolic ideals that were posited with Keble's assistance in the first volume of the *Tracts for the Times*.[22] Keble, Newman, and Froude envisioned a clergy that was completely detached from the aristocratic powers in the church, one that would obey the episcopate as Keble had urged in his first contribution to the tracts. Such obedience to the bishops would prove the "safest way" for the clergy in times of political change, and by liberating itself from the upper classes (who controlled many of the livings), the clergy would assist in restoring the lost popularity of the English church with the people.

---

[21] *The Autobiography of Isaac Williams,* (London: Thomas Nelson, 1963) 113; for Pusey's part in the original Oxford Movement, see *Apologia Pro Vita Sua*, 77-79; also John Griffin, "Dr. Pusey and the Oxford Movement," *Historical Magazine of the Protestant Episcopal Church* 42 (June 1973): 137-39.

[22] One of the minor Tractarians, William Copeland, wrote to Dean Church on this subject: "A parsonage in these days becomes a temptation, perhaps to be resisted. . . . As time goes on there will be many repenting of their smug parsonage houses." 7 November 1840, Hamilton Collection, Pusey House, Oxford. See also John Griffin, "The Social Implications of the Oxford Movement," *Historical Magazine of the Protestant Episcopal Church* 45 (June 1975): 155-66.

Keble gradually separated himself from the ideology of the first revival, and by 1835 he was critical of Froude for many of his "young" ideas. Newman observed the change in Keble, and with the death of Hurrell Froude early in 1836 he was left as the sole possessor of the original idea of complete independence for the English church.

The *Lyra Apostolica*

The Oxford Movement had little to do directly with literature, but there was one volume of poetry produced by the Keble group in 1836, The Lyra Apostolica. We can measure the original hopes of the apostolicals by looking at this volume, and we can also measure the early opposition that developed against the revival by the conservatives at Oxford.

Samuel Wilberforce, for example, wrote of the volume in *The British Critic:*". . . the mind of the composer(s) had probably lived too much apart from the tenderness and sympathies of domestic life."[23]

Wilberforce complained of the radical tendencies in the *Lyra* and reminded his readers that all the great poets, unlike the authors of this volume, were conservatives; and he did not care for the "harsh and rash versification" of the collection. There were other complaints against the volume, but it sold reasonably well.

Most of the poems in the collection, numbering a hundred and seventy-five in total, had been published earlier in the conservative journal *The British Magazine*. Newman's compromise include more than half of the total collection, and most of his had been published before the Movement was underway.

Keble's poems seem to have been especially written for the occasion, and we should note that Keble shared in the original impulse of the volume—to demonstrate a new kind of religion to English churchmen, one that was completely independent of the state and as far from the Protestantism of the day as from Roman Catholicism.

---

[23]Samuel Wilberforce, "Sacred Poetry," *British Critic* 21 (January 1837): 168.

The *Lyra,* like the first *Tracts for the Times,* was aimed as a kind of satire against the conservatives then prevalent in the Church of England. The intent of the poems can often be grasped from the titles—for example, "Liberalism," "Conservatism," "Protestantism," "Suppression of the Irish See." Apart from the religious merits of the poems, they are good enough to warrant attention only by advanced specialists of the Victorian period.

Keble does not use allegory in his contributions (see note 24), and there is no reference to Nature or children in his poems. The *Lyra* aimed at stirring up the reader to an awareness of high-church traditions in the Church of England. As Walter Lock has noted,

> The spirit which stirred him found vent once more in the po-etry—in the poems of the Lyra Apostolica—how different from those of the Christian Year! Rugged, austere, wanting the old melody, yet with a ring of the battle trumpet through them, they breathe defiance. . . . [24]

The object of the defiance was the conservative, Erastian Prot-estant Church of England. There is deliberately an avoidance of any of the literary graces and any indirect allusions or meta-phors. The image of God in these poems is almost harsh, and the consoling features of the Christian faith are given up for an al-most apocalyptic view of the church.

In addition, there are repeated attacks on the state-church al-liance, the low spiritual life of the bishops and clergy, and the wealth of the church. Several of the poems hold up, as examples of the indifferent bishops of the day, the Greek bishops of the Primitive Church (third and fourth centuries). Taken as a whole, the *Lyra Apostolica* is radical poetry at its best, and it is easy to understand why it was not well received at Oxford, "the capital of Toryism."

We can see the method of Keble's radicalism at work in one of his most celebrated poems, "Let Us Depart Hence." Walter Lock has cited the lines without giving the critical lines that follow the above. The poem is given in full.

------

[24]Walter Lock, *John Keble: A Biography* (London: Methuen & Co., 1893) 78-79.

Is there no sound about our Altars heard
> *Of gliding forms that long have watched in vain*
For slumbering discipline to break her chain,
And aim the bolt by Theodosius feared:
"Let us depart;"—these English souls are seared,
> *Who for one grasp of perishable gold,*
> *Would brave the course by holy men of old*
Laid on the robbers of the shrines they reared;
> *Who shout for joy to see the ruffian band*
Come to reform, where ne'er they came to pray,
> *E'en where, unbidden, Seraphs never trod.*
Let us depart, and leave the apostate land
> *To meet the rising whirlwind as she may,*
Without her guardian Angels and her God.

Lock, and most Anglo-Catholic scholars, have not noticed the solution that Keble and his friends posed for the question of non-Anglicans reforming the Church of England. Keble advised that the apostolicals should "depart," that is, break with the Establishment (exactly the solution that Newman and Froude were advising) through nonresistance to state efforts to break the alliance.

The argument of the poem is relatively simple, and it is given as an answer to the question that occupies the opening quatrain of the sonnet. It can be paraphrased in the following way: Is there no protest in the church for those who have patiently waited for the revival of church discipline, especially the rite of excommunication? Has the power of the state deprived the church of all its discipline? If this is so, churchmen should separate from the State itself, for the English were overwhelmed by the love of gold and would risk the curse of excommunication that had, in earlier times, been aimed at the persecutors of the church. The English shout for joy to see the various ruffians have a say in reforming the church even though they were not members of it. These robbers of the church go into even the most sacred area of the church, its teaching, a place where even angels would be fearful to tread. Let all good churchmen oppose such meddling in church matters by breaking with the Establishment and even England itself. Skepticism will probably overwhelm the "apostate" nation without the assistance of her churchmen and God.

There are several difficult allusions in the sonnet. In the fourth line, for example, there is a reference to Theodosius, a Roman emperor and convert to Christianity in the late fourth century. What is relevant about Theodosius is that he enforced Christianity as the official religion of the Empire—and punitive measures against heretics—an ideal for Keble. From the Keble poem it appears that even Theodosius was reluctant to invoke the rite of excommunication ("the bolt").

In the thirteenth line of the poem, Keble used the phrase "rising whirlwind" as a metaphor for the growing spread of infidelity that was the great religious problem of the day. The state, Keble argued, could never resist the problem without the assistance of the "apostolic" church. It is difficult to know with any exactness who the "holy men of old" were, unless Keble was referring to some of the militant bishops of the primitive and medieval church who furiously resisted efforts by the state to seize church property.

The themes of the *Lyra Apostolica* were fairly well shown in the brief excerpts cited: separation from the state, reform of the lower clergy, and an opposition to conservatism and Protestantism.

The poems are perhaps not the best kind of poetry, and it would strain a reader's belief to be told that they are to be included among the hidden masterpieces of the nineteenth century.

Still, the *Lyra Apostolica* is one of those rare works in which an idea is vitally present in the work without overwhelming the art itself. The poems are well constructed; the vocabulary is fresh and yet not academic or archaic. They stimulate the reader without intimidating him. The collection, as a whole, has a rich variety of forms and presents some of the best poetry that Keble and his friends ever wrote. It might be noted here that one of Newman's most celebrated works, "Lead Kindly Light," was included in the *Lyra*.

Aftermath

Keble did not maintain the ideals of 1833 or the *Lyra Apostolica* for any great length of time. In the years after Froude's death (February 1836) we see Keble moving slowly into the conservative camp. He became a "Z," an establishment man. But for a brief period he had been something else, and during the brief period he inspired a younger friend with a zeal that is revered in our day. Shortly after Newman became a Catholic, he wrote to Keble,

> To you I owe it, humanly speaking, that I am what and where I am. Others have influenced me in various ways, but not one can I name but you, among those I ever knew, except one who is gone [Froude], who has had any part in setting my face in that special direction which has led me to my present inestimable gain.[25]

Keble was not happy with the Newman letter, and in the years after 1845 he tried to keep persons from following in Newman's steps. The ultimate kindness that Newman performed for Keble was to sharply edit the letters he donated to Keble College in 1878. Such a gesture should remind us that Keble must have had some problems with his place in the Church of England about which we can now only speculate. One might only regret that Keble did not act with greater charity towards Newman.

Conclusion

In this chapter I have challenged many of the existing studies on Keble and the Oxford Movement. Against the almost overwhelming authority of Anglo-Catholic historians of the Oxford Movement, it was argued that Newman's description of John Keble as the "true and primary . . . author" of the Oxford Movement could be validated through a new reading of "National Apostasy" and an analysis of Keble's correspondence of 1827 to 1834. Far from being an old-fashioned and traditional Tory clergyman, Keble was a gifted though somewhat naive innovator whose ideas inspired the most important phase of English ecclesiastical history since the Reformation.

Such an interpretation goes some length to defend Keble and his friends from the charge of secular historians that they were a self-seeking group of hysterical young men who were primarily intent on defending the various privileges of the English church. The "apostolicals," at least in 1833, were as opposed to many of

---

[25]Dessain, *Letters and Diaries of John Henry Newman*, 11:34.

those privileges as the various writers for the *Westminster Review*. My reading of "National Apostasy" and the *Tracts for the Times* could be documented far more extensively than I have attempted in this chapter. The great wonder is that most of this material has been ignored by the many scholars working on either Keble or the Oxford Movement. The radical implications of the first volume of the tracts are fairly obvious, as are its implications for the clergy. The type of Anglican clergyman as envisioned by Jane Austen or Anthony Trollope would eventually become less prominent once a separation from the state and upper classes was effected. Far from seeking to attack the English middle classes for their "mammonism," the first Tractarians wanted to make the church more accessible to both the middle and lower classes, as befitted its Catholic character. Newman was deadly earnest when he wished a spoilation of goods upon the English bishops in the first of the tracts, but even he did not go as far as Keble in 1833, for it was Keble who described such an attack on the wealth of the English church as "wholesome."

The ideology of 1833, then, was revolutionary in its meaning, and there was good reason for one of the Oxford Conservatives to complain that the early tracts would "frighten men."[26] Yet if the church were forced to give up the protection provided by the state, it still retained a far more important source of leadership. Each of the early Tractarians was fully committed to the idea of obedience to the bishops, for the episcopate would provide the only bond of unity once the alliance with the state was broken. However, when the bishops condemned *Tract 90* and the Catholic claims put forward by the "apostolicals," as they did in 1841 and 1842, the Keble party responded by more or less ignoring the bishops. It was not just Dr. Pusey who was opposed by the whole of the episcopate. All of those who shared Pusey's doctrines in one degree or another were under the same condemnation, and foremost in that collection of "Puseyites" was John Keble.

---

[26]William Palmer to Newman, September 1833, CP.

Yet the party of Anglo-Catholics, led by Keble and Pusey, grew much stronger in the second half of the nineteenth century. Keble was not as active as Dr. Pusey in his writings on behalf of the Catholic principle of Anglicanism, but Pusey could scarcely have achieved his many triumphs on behalf of that principle without Keble's support. By the end of the century, the English Catholics had become a legitimate and powerful force in the Church of England.

Chapter V

The Final Years:
Crisis and Compromise

The *Lyra Innocentium*

Keble's literary work came to an end in 1846 with the publication of the *Lyra Innocentium*. The second volume is a collection
of lyric poems written between 1842 and 1845, which Keble wrote
to console himself for the disaster of Newman's conversion.

> I have got a scheme for raising money for the church . . . to pub-
> lish a set of things which have been accumulating for the last 3
> or 4 years. . . . It has been a great comfort to me in the desolating
> anxiety of the last two years, and I wish I could settle at once to
> some other task.[1]

As it turned out, some of the editor's comments on the poems in
the *Lyra* probably increased Keble's anxiety about the English
church; but the poetry serves as a kind of apologia for Keble's faith
in the church and why he would never leave that church. The
theme of remaining in the church is so obvious that it is curious
that Coleridge, as editor and generous reviewer of the *Lyra,* did

---

[1]Keble to Coleridge, 14 August 1845, CC.

not mention it. Later, Coleridge devoted a whole chapter in his *Memoir* of Keble to the background of the *Lyra* and the problem created by some of the poems.

> We all agreed in our admiration of then, and also in the token they gave that Keble had advanced considerably in his religious opinions. On grounds partly of actual disagreement, and partly of the imprudence . . . of publishing them at that critical time, we objected to the insertion of two or three of the poems.[2]

The critical time was of course Newman's conversion, which Keble had been anticipating for at least three years. Issac Williams must have known of Keble's anxiety over that event, yet he did not mention it in his account of the writing of the *Lyra*.

> . . . a conversation of this kind gave rise to the "Lyra Innocentium," for Keble said he thought of altering the "Christian Year" to adapt it to his present views. "Well," I said, "if you do, we have the former, and we will ourselves reprint it and keep to it. If you want to express your altered views, write another book, and then we can still keep to the old." About the same time, on looking at John Edward, his godson, then an infant, he said, "Why should not the idea inspire you to write a book of poems about it?" These thoughts and conversations at Bisley . . . gave rise to the "Lyra Innocentium."[3]

The writing of the poems may have consoled Keble, but in the ensuing controversy over "Mother Out of Sight" Keble's problems with the Church of England increased. The poem, with its praise of Mary, was too controversial for publication in 1846. Newman's conversion had confirmed the Evangelical suspicion that the Oxford Movement was a popish plot and, while the Anglo-Catholic community had united to discredit Newman, the suspicion remained. The crisis of Newman's conversion was made more difficult by the anti-Catholic agitation against the continued funding of Maynooth (a Jesuit college) in 1845.

Protestant Anglicans charged that Rome sanctioned idolatry in its homage to the Blessed Virgin; therefore, no funding should

---

[2]John T. Coleridge, *A Memoir of the Rev. John Keble* (Oxford: James Parker, 1868) 296.

[3]*The Autobiography of Isaac Williams,* 117

be allowed for a church that taught "the worship of the Virgin Mary."[4] Keble's "Mother Out of Sight," suggested Coleridge, would increase the Protestant suspicions of their principles. But Keble's greatest problem came with the views of his friends, Coleridge and the Dysons. The latter suggested that there was nothing at all distinctive about Mary. Coleridge did not agree with the Dysons' view, but he believed that Keble had gone too far in the other direction. After much soul-searching that Coleridge did not mention, Keble gave in, but not without a brief protest against his friends.

> I should not be candid, if I were not to own to you that as far as I can remember and understand myself, no one thing has seemed to me to tell so much against our Church, as your scruples and those of the Dysons, on . . . the B. [lessed] Virgin.[5]

In another letter Keble described his difficulties at greater length.

> I am sure I ought to share in your feeling, that is not for those to be judging between different Churches who have made such ill use, as I for one have, of present helps to holiness . . . but it keeps coming unpleasantly before me that this is hardly consistent with the Priest's office; and especially when, as sometimes happens, I am asked for advice, then indeed I have to think of the blind leading the blind.[6]

If the matter were not so serious, an ironic humor could be found in this debate between Keble and his editors, for the *Lyra Innocentium* was intended to serve as a testament to Keble's faith in the Church of England.

The first lesson of the *Lyra* is the moral obligation of Anglicans to remain in the church of their baptism. In illustrating that idea Keble offered a new interpretation of Nature. In *The Christian Year* the example of created Nature served as proof, by analogy, of the existence of God: the reader was led upward through a contemplation of Nature's beauty to a contemplation with love

---

[4]Quoted in *Anti-Catholicism in Victorian England,* ed. Edward Norman (London: Barnes and Noble Co., 1968) 33.

[5]Keble to Coleridge, October 1845, CC.

[6]Ibid., January 1846, CC.

of the Author of Nature. In the *Lyra,* one of the more dominant images presented by Nature was that of hiding and trusting, rather than inquiring. From "Lessons of Nature":

> *Hast thou no wisdom here to learn,*
> *Thou nestling of the Holy Dove,*
> *How hearts that with the true life burn*
> *Live by the pulse of filial love?*
>
> ....
>
> *Think of yon brood, yon downy breast,*
> *And hid thee deep in Jesus' will.*

If one could live by the "pulse of filial love," difficulties in the church would vanish. Those who failed in that virtue were of course the converts of 1845, whom Keble in another poem likened to "doubting Thomases." In another poem from the series on Nature in the *Lyra,* Keble is even more direct in his advice:

> *Look how the hen invites her brood*
> *Beneath her wing to lie,*
> *Look how she calls them to their food,*
> *How eyes, in eager, dauntless mood,*
> *The wheeling hawk on high*
>
> ....
>
> *But be thou gathered;—one and all*
> *Those simple nestlings see,*
> *How hurrying at their mother's call,*
> *To their own home, what'er befall,*
> *In faith entire they flee.*

In numerous other poems. Keble invokes the idea that the simple duty of Anglicans is to shelter themselves within the church:

> *And Christ hath lowly hearts, that rest*
> *Mid fallen Salem's rush and strife:*
> *The pure, peace-loving breast*
> *E'en here can find her life.*

There are two other poems that reflect the same idea, but offer a more direct criticism of the recent converts or any who might be thinking of going over. In "Disuse of Excommunication" Keble expressed his regret that the idea of excommunication had not been exercised by the modern church, and the following lines indicate why Keble thought the rite of excommunication useful at the time.

> O wondrous warfare of the Spouse of God,
> Trampled to earth, yet wielding bolts so keen,
> She dares not hurl them in her wrath abroad,
> Only their ireful lustre glares half-seen.
> For if she once unlock her quivered store,
>
> Once speak the words that in her bosom dwell,
> Earth could not bear the sound; the anguish sore
> Might drive her haughtiest to the scourge and cell.

The Church of England is of course the "spouse of God," and the power of excommunication had always been in the church, though it was "half-seen." But who was to be the object of excommunication? The rite or process of excommunication was hardly characteristic of the English church. It might be that Keble was speaking in general terms, or obliquely against some of the more liberal bishops or politicians of the day, but the topical references throughout the *Lyra* suggest a "safer" object. The poem may have been addressed to the recent converts, including Newman.

Keble certainly believed that there was a great sin in their leaving the church, and he later quoted with approval the strong letter of the bishops against the converts.[7] His correspondence from 1845 through a much later period overflows with caustic remarks about those who had gone over, and it is unlikely that Keble, in 1845 at least, would be willing to stir up any more difficulties in the church. Keble's resentment of the converts has already been noted, and he did take a significant part in the high-church effort to keep those who might be wavering in their loyalty to the English church, partly by slandering the converts and by exaggerating the dangers of the Roman system. If there is anything ecumenical in Keble's conduct or statement during that period, it was generally lost on those who knew him best.

There is one final poem in the *Lyra* that might be briefly discussed—the first poem in the collection, "To All Friendly Read-

---

[7]"London Union on Church Matters," *Guardian,* 21 October 1850, 1179.

ers." I have delayed my discussion of this poem because it is almost impossible to understand the work without reference to the historical and autobiographical themes presented in the work. The poem is quoted almost in full.

> There are, who love upon their knees
> To linger when their prayers are said,
> And lengthen out their litanies,
> In duteous care for quick and dead
> Thou, of all Love the Source and Guide;
> O may some hovering thought of theirs,
> While I am kneeling, gently guide,
> And higher waft these earth-bound prayers.
>
> There are, who gazing on the stars
> Love-tokens read from worlds of light,
> Not as dim-seen through prison-bars,
> But as with Angels welcome bright.
> O had we kept entire the vow
> And covenant of our infant eyes,
> We too might trace untrembling now
> Glad lessons on the moonlight skies.
>
> What if there were one, who laid a hand
> Upon the Lyre of Innocence,
> While the other, over sea and land
> Beckoned foul shapes, in dream intense
> Of earthly passion? Whoso reads,
> In pity kneel for him, and pour
> A deep-heart prayer (O! much it needs)
> That lies may be his hope no more.
>
> Pray that the mist, by sin and shame
> Left on his soul, may flee; that he
> A true and timely word may frame
> For weary hearts, that ask to see
> Their way in our dim twilight hour;
> His lips are purged with penance-fire,
> That he may guide them, in Christ's power,
> Along the path of their desire;
>
> And with no faint nor erring voice
> May to the wanderer whisper, Stay:
> God chooses for thee; seal His choice,
> Nor from thy Mother's shadow stray;

For sure thine holy Mother's shade
Rests yet upon thine ancient home:
No voice from Heaven hath clearly said,
"Let us depart;" then fear to roam.

Pray thou the Prayer of Innocents
On Earth, of Saints in Heaven above,
Guard, as of old, our lonely tents;
Till, as one Faith is ours, in Love
We own all Churches, and are owned,—
Pray Him to save, by Chastenings keen,
The harps that hail His Bride enthroned
From wayward touch of hands unclean.

The context of "To All Friendly Readers" suggests that Keble was attempting to do his best to keep members of the Anglo-Catholic party from following Newman, but there are numerous difficulties in evaluating Keble's image of the church. In the first stanza Keble made brief mention of prayers for "quick and dead," which faintly suggests the value of praying for the dead. Anglicans rightly understood that prayers for the dead inferred at least the doctrine of purgatory, and they were highly critical of such a doctrine. The final stanza in the poem contains the line "We own all Churches and are owned," which does suggest an ecumenical view of the relations between Rome and Canterbury. It is ironic that Keble should have included such a line, for he used the exclusive claims of the Roman church as one of many reasons to keep others away from Rome.[8]

The argument of staying in the Church of England, moreover, was the most consistent theme in Keble's apologetic. "God chooses for thee: seal his choice, / Nor from thy Mother's shadow stray." No circumstances would warrant anyone from leaving the church: "No voice from Heaven hath clearly said, / 'Let us depart;' then fear to roam." Those who did go over had failed and lost the gift of innocence: A dutiful child would never consider taking such a

---

[8]John Keble, *Sermons, Occasional and Academical* 2nd ed. (Oxford: James Parker, 1848) 313: "Undoubtedly it is so, when any one section of the true Church calls itself Christian, Catholic, Evangelical, or the like, to the exclusion of the rest."

step. As Newman observed in his review of the *Lyra Innocentium,*

> Well would it be for all men, could they always live the life they
> lived as infants, possessed of the privileges, not the responsibil-
> ities of regeneration.[9]

J. T. Coleridge also wrote a review of the *Lyra Innocentium.*
One of the themes in his review was that the faith of the author
of *The Christian Year* was substantially the same one faith found
in the poetry of 1846.[10] But the two volumes are, as Coleridge
knew, dramatically different. The reform motif of the earlier volume is absent in the *Lyra,* and a careful reader notices that Keble
has placed himself in the role of one who was appointed to serve
as a "guide" to others. Thus, the "mantle of authority," which Keble's critics and admirers ascribed to him, was consciously assumed by Keble.

The *Lyra Innocentium* was Keble's most honorable response
to the threat of massive conversion to Rome. Newman rightly
understood that the poetry was directed against him and those
who might be thinking of going over under the category of children who did not "trust their elders." The converts, according to
Keble, were deficient in purity of "heart and mind" and guilty of
being "doubting Thomases" in their questioning of the Catholic
claims of the Church of England. If, as a recent scholar has suggested, Newman's essay on Keble's *Lyra* represents the "last
word" on the Oxford Movement,[11] a whole new image of Keble and
the Oxford Movement is required. Keble's loyalty to the English
church is best explained by his use of a series of lines from Wordsworth's "Stock Dove".

> *O dearest boy, dearest boy! my heart*
> *For better lore would seldom yearn,*

---

[9]John Henry Newman, "John Keble," in *Essays, Critical and Historical* (London: Longman's, Green, & CO., 1878) 2:432.

[10]John Taylor Coleridge, "Sacred Poetry—*Lyra Innocentium,*"
Quarterly Review 78 (June 1846): 23-45.

[11]George B. Tennyson, *Victorian Devotional Poetry: The Tractarian
Mode*(Berkeley CA: University of California Press, 1981) 196.

Could I but teach the hundredth part
Of what from thee I learn.[12]

Even this brief extract from "Stock Dove" provides a basic clue to Keble's technique of putting aside all controversy within and without the English church. Brian W. Martin has commented on Keble's debt to Wordsworth.

> In Wordsworth's poem the adult tries to force the boy to rationalise his preference for Kilve rather than Liswyn Farn. The boy is unable, or unwilling to do this, and finally, in order to satisfy the adult, casts around for some explanation that will stand as a reason for the insistent adult. He sees the weather-vane on Liswyn Farn and gives it as a negative reason for preferring Kilve by the sea-shore. The point, however, that Wordsworth was making, was that the boy's feelings for a place should have been sufficient for the adult: There was no need for reasons.[13]

Feelings of place, duty, and loyalty were sufficient in themselves, according to Keble and Wordsworth, and those feelings kept Keble of the Church of England.

Hampden and Gorham

In 1847 Renn Hampden was nominated to an episcopal see by Lord John Russell. The gesture was of course aimed at the Tractarians who had opposed Hampden in a far less serious capacity twelve years earlier. Protestant Anglicans rejoiced in the Russell appointment and called Russell a "friend to God and man" for his courage.[14] Hampden denied that he had been a Socinian or ever written anything against Revelation, but one of the most important proofs of his orthodoxy was in his reminder that those who had opposed him were now Roman Catholics.[15]

---

[12]In Brian W. Martin, *John Keble: Priest, Professor and Poet* (London: Croom Helm, 1976) 81-82.

[13]Ibid.

[14]Lord Ashley to Lord John Russell, 8 April 1847, Russell Papers, Public Records Office, London.

[15]Renn Hampden to Lord John Russell, May 1847: "Where is Mr. Newman now?" Russell Papers of 1850, Public Records Office, London.

Keble had already passed thorough his own crisis with the English bishops, and it is not quite accurate to suggest that the Tractarian respect for the episcopate began to decline within the Hampden affair.[16] Many years later, Pusey noted that one of the critical points of difference between himself and Newman was in their respective attitudes towards the English bishops.

> Single bishops . . . do not commit the Church. . . . Dear J. H. N. said to me one day at Littlemore, "Pusey, we have leant on the bishops, and they have given way under us." Dear J. K. and I never did lean on the bishops, but on the Church. We, or rather the whole Church have had plenty of scandals as to bishops.[17]

Parts of the above are simply false, for Pusey himself had defined as one of the notes of "Puseyism" an allegiance to the episcopal office;[18] and of course the basic theme of the first Oxford Movement had been to get the bishops to assume their legitimate power, versus that of the state, in the church. Yet the remarks do serve to illustrate the growing isolation of the Anglo-Catholics within their own church and the increased distance that separated them from Rome.

Keble wrote almost nothing about the debate over the appointment of Hampden; but he did publish a new edition of his sermons in 1847 that serves as a personal manifesto on why English Catholics in the Church of England should not have been bothered by the appointment. In the preface to the sermons he returned to the argument of the *Lyra:* Good Anglicans should ignore problems in the church as much as possible. If the humiliations of English church history could not be avoided, loyal Anglicans go by the advice of others. A dutiful child should to be content with the kind of parents and home that had been given to him by God, and it was sinful to quarrel or complain about one's

---

[16]Charles P. Clarke, *The Oxford Movement and After* (London: A. R. Mowbray Co., 1932) 148.

[17]Harry P. Liddon, *Life of the Rev. E. B. Pusey,* 4 vols. (London: Macmillan and Co., 1898) 4:231.

[18]Owen Chadwick, ed., *The Mind of the Oxford Movement,* (Stanford CA: Stanford University Press, 1960) 51.

birth. No one should go over to Rome without evidence that was "almost miraculous" in character; and those who had gone over were guilty of pride and intellectual restlessness. The "safer way" was to remain in the church, for the Roman church was still the church of idolators and other evils. The various forms of Roman idolatry would be presented to the convert for his "express sanction."[19]

The Gorham Trial

The Gorham verdict of 1850 might be interpreted as the very kind of event that would fall under Keble's description as "almost miraculous" in the problems it created for Catholic-minded clergy in the English church. In January of 1850, when the Gorham verdict was still pending, Keble wrote to Henry Wilberforce about its meaning: "It seems to me as if the existence of the English Church as a *Church,* is at stake."[20] George Cornelius Gorham was an evangelical clergyman whose denial of the doctrine of baptismal regeneration had caused Bishop Henry Phillpotts to refuse him a living in his diocese. Gorham was somewhat unlucky in his conflict with Phillpotts because many of the bishops held views on the disputed doctrine similar to his own. When Gorham took his case to the episcopal court, he lost; then he took his case to the civil court, the Privy Council, and won. The court declared that the doctrine of baptismal regeneration was an "open question" in the church and that no clergyman could be excluded from a living because he denied the doctrine.

Keble was deeply agitated by the trial and published a series of pamphlets in 1850 on its implications. The argument of this material illustrates an aspect of Keble's thought that was briefly mentioned earlier in this study—his intellectual debt to the reformation settlement of the sixteenth century. Keble endorsed Royal Supremacy as established by Henry VIII. His grievance of

---

[19]Keble, *Sermons, Occasional and Academical,* 316: "Image worship . . . the worship of the Blessed Virgin and the Saints are presented to the convent for his express sanction."

[20]Keble to Henry Wilberforce, 23 January 1850, Papers of William H. Mill, 1846-1853, Lambeth Palace Library, London.

1850 was that the Privy Council represented a departure from the original terms of Royal Supremacy.

> I do not deny that the Church of England did both really and formally admit the Regal Supremacy, as was claimed by King Henry VIII and Queen Elizabeth. It virtually therefore bound itself to submission to the Court of Delegates itself, *as then established and constituted.*[21]

Thus, whatever the Privy Council might rule on the doctrine was not binding on the church.

> Our consciences, then, are quite clear of any obligations by his engagement to receive the doctrinal decisions of the Privy Council as part of the doctrine of the Church. No number nor amount of them can make the Church of England formally heretical, nor bind us to withdraw from her ministrations . . . we are just doing what our rulers, from Henry and Elizabeth downwards, have directed us to do.[22]

The basic flaw in the Privy Council was that there were two non-Anglicans serving on it. The presence of the non-Anglican element meant that Keble and his coreligionists in the Anglo-Catholic party could ignore any of its decisions with which they disagreed.

Yet Keble was more disturbed than the material in the pamphlets of 1850 would suggest. Most of the members of the party signed a petition to the effect that the English church would lose its claim to be regarded as a branch of the universal Catholic church if the decision were not rejected by the church. According to Manning, who signed the petition and then in consequence of his signature went over to Rome in 1851, it was at this time Keble made the celebrated remark, "If the Church of England were to fail altogether, you will find it at Hursley."[23] I contend that Keble meant exactly what he said. He was the exponent of the Cath-

---

[21]John Keble, "Trial of Doctrine," in *Occasional Papers and Reviews,* ed. Harry Liddon (Oxford: James Parker, 1877) 207.

[22]Ibid., 210.

[23]Quoted in Edmund Purcell, *Life of Cardinal Manning,* 2 vols. (London: Macmillan's, 1896)2:254.

olic principle of the Church of England, against many if not all of his bishops, his fellow-clergy, the greater majority of the laity, and against Rome. It is in Keble's solitary exposition of what he called "the true English Church" and the "true Catholic sacramental religion."[24] What preserved Keble for the Church of England was scarcely the "perfect confidence" in its teachings or a belief that Newman's conversion was a providential act that was destined to bring the two churches closer together. Rather, Keble's hatred of Rome, an inheritance derived through his father and extending back to the Reformation itself, was his last defense of the English church. The converts of the day were like the converts of every period since the Reformation: they deteriorated in a moral sense as soon as they crossed the Tiber. In a sermon of several years earlier Keble raised this theme:

> Is there one single instance, since the heat of the Reformation was over, of any person passing from the English church to any Church . . . and afterwards becoming at all remarkable for sanctity? . . . On the other hand, there are, we know, fearful examples of the final results of a man's encouraging in himself that craving of mind which commonly leads to conversion.[25]

Throughout the writings and correspondence of 1850, Keble regarded any softening on the Roman question as the "worst sign of our day."[26] He quoted with approval the episcopal declaration that those who went over to Rome were guilty of "an act of schism"[27] and privately did his best to prevent such events.

The correspondence with Robert Wilberforce illustrates Keble's method, for what he was saying in his letters was often a paraphrase of what he had already written.

> I trust, dear friend, that you are not allowing yourself to look out

---

[24]"Letter to the Parishioners of Hursley," in Liddon, *Occasional Papers and Reviews*, 245.

[25]Keble, "Endurance of Church Imperfections," *Sermons, Occasional and Academical,*318.

[26]Keble to Pusey, 18 October 1850, Keble-Pusey Correspondence, vol. 3, Pusey House, Oxford.

[27]Ibid., 18 December 1850.

for the worst possible construction of what is said and done in our church. That would be very unlike the R. W. whom I used to know.[28]

The Gorham verdict was no more than an "imperfection" in the church, and corruption in one part of the church did not mean that the whole was corrupted. The difficulties in the Roman system were at least equal to difficulties within the Church of England. Keble would allow no reason to cause a man to go over to Rome, no matter what might be taking place in the English church. Thus when another state trial of doctrine was about to be concluded, he wrote to J. T. Coleridge,

> No doubt, as you say, there is a tendency in all this to drive unstable, indeed, less settled than the loosest possible tooth, if such matters can cough them out from among us. For what is it to the proof or disproof of the Pope's Supremacy, or the *ruling* powers of the B. V. M., whether I may have a cross on the Altar table or not? Though I must add, I do expect that when these outward signs are suppressed, the Truth itself which they symbolize will be openly persecuted and probably forbidden to be taught in the Established Church.[29]

Keble never got over the idea that those who had gone over to Rome were guilty of a serious moral transgression. Yet he also refused to put his own faith into any kind of coherent form that an outsider could understand. He opposed "mere Protestantism" and "ultra-Protestantism," while defending several of those most important qualities in both: anti-Romanism and the rights of private judgment. Catholics sometimes complained that Keble had narrowed the terms and exponents of Catholic orthodoxy to an exceedingly small number of Anglican clergymen in the mid-Victorian church, and suggested that such a process was scarcely Catholic in its characteristics or implications. If Keble felt any difficulties with his position, those difficulties were easier to endure than what the Roman church demanded.

---

[28]David Newsome, *The Parting of Friends* (Cambridge: Harvard University Press, 1966) 396.

[26]Keble to Coleridge, 11 December 1855, CC.

Conclusion

Historians of the second phase of the Oxford Movement usually take an optimistic view of the various achievements of Keble, Pusey, and others in the Anglo-Catholic party. Of the three originals in the Oxford Movement, only Newman went over to Rome; Keble and Pusey remained loyal to the church of their baptism. Through their loyalty, perseverance, and sanctity they inspired several generations to suffer on behalf of the Catholic principle of Anglicanism. From a small and badly fragmented group in 1845, led by Keble and Pusey, the moment it emerged as the dominant party in the Church of England.[1] "Puseyism" became a term of honor so great that on the occasion of Pusey's death, one of the Anglo-Catholic newspapers could proclaim that when the term *Puseyism* was correctly understood, it meant all that was the finest in the teachings of the Church of England.[2]

John Keble, almost as much as Pusey himself, was a spokesman for a creed that was known to critics and friends alike as

---

[1]Eugene Fairweather, introduction to *The Oxford Movement* (Oxford: Oxford University Press, 1964) 7.

[2]"Dr. Pusey's Death," *Guardian,* 22 August 1822.

"Puseyism." There are reasons to suggest that several of the most important items in Pusey's vision of the Church of England were taken from John Keble. Apropos of my argument, it might be noted that two of Dr. Pusey's most important works from the post-1845 years were addressed to John Keble, and in each we find much that can be traced to the writings of Keble. The first was Pusey's "Letter to John Keble," published in the *English Churchman* shortly after Newman's conversion; the second was the *Eirenicon: A Letter to the Author of 'The Christian Year,'* 1865. Both works have been interpreted as gestures of the ecumenical spirit that was nurtured by Keble and Pusey in the second phase of the movement. Newman and the other converts received much abuse from the Anglican community, but none from the Anglo-Catholic party. A spirit of openness and friendly neutrality towards Rome came to be one of the leading characteristics of the party in its later history.[3] Newman's move did not divest him of many of the finer qualities of Anglicanism, and the loyalty of Keble and Pusey served to create a bridge between the two churches leading up to the eirenicon of 1865 and the ecumenical negotiations of the present day. There were important differences between Newman and those whom he had left behind, but the spirit of friendly neutrality that was enhanced by the spirit of Christian charity on both sides enabled them to engage in a friendly dialogue with mutual trust and confidence in 1865. None of that would have been possible without Pusey's "Letter to John Keble" of 1845.[4]

Such an interpretation, I believe, does not do justice to the zeal for the cause of Catholic Anglicanism that was so characteristic of both men, nor does that interpretation do justice to what Keble and Pusey actually wrote on the subject of "Romanism," the converts, or the "Church of Rome." Neither Keble nor Pusey ever de-

---

[3]Thomas Allchin, "The *Via Media*—An Anglican Reevaluation," in *Newman: A Portrait Restored,* ed. John Coulson and Thomas Allchin (London: Sheed and Ward, 1967) 69.

[4]Roderick Strange, "Reflections on a Controversy: Newman and Pusey's *Eirenicon,*" in *Pusey Rediscovered,* ed. Perry Butler (London: S. P. C. K., 1983) 332-48.

scribed the Roman church as "Catholic"; and from the writings of each, we can conclude that they were united in believing that Romanism had its own problems, equal to anything in the Church of England. Indeed, I believe that the most consistent feature in what was called "Puseyism" was anti-Romanism. It is worth remarking that few of Pusey's friends ever considered him soft on that issue, and so it was with Keble—perhaps even more so. When Samuel Wilberforce was doing his part to diminish the effects of Pusey's ministry in his diocese, he noted that Keble's disciples, unlike those of Pusey, did not go over to Rome; and while that praise was reversed after the Gorham verdict, it is true that Pusey had a much poorer record with prospective converts than Keble. Yet Keble knew that Pusey's ministry, however Romish it might appear, was designed to prevent people from following Newman's example. He defended Pusey by describing him as a chicken being followed by a flock of ducklings.[5] Without Pusey's ministry, there would have been an even greater number of converts.

By way of illustrating Keble's and Pusey's efforts to retain persons in the Church of England, it is worth examining what Pusey, with Keble's support, wrote in his "Letter" and eirenicon and what others said about both works. Newman, who was the object of both works, knew that they were designed to discredit him and whatever he might say about the reasons for his leaving the English church. The first was an argument that it was Newman's "solitary genius," which the English church could not understand or nurture, that had led him to Rome. That letter was the result of a series of meetings, between Pusey and Keble and others in the Anglo-Catholic party, on the proper form of response to Newman's move, whenever it was to come. In his correspondence of 1843 through the date of his conversion, Newman had let people know that he was going over—it was just a matter of time. Keble said in a letter several months before the conversion that Newman had not been a loyal Anglican for at least five years. Yet Keble and Pusey were willing to persevere, whereas

---

[5]Reginald D. Wilberforce, *Life of Samuel Wilberforce,* 3 vols. (London: John Murray, 1881) 2:95.

Newman was not; and thus the legend that it was Newman's "sensitivity" that led him to Rome was born. When the "thunderbolt" took place, Keble was ill for two weeks. He admitted that Newman had become "practically dead" as far as he was concerned, and he did not feel up to reading the *Essay on Development* for a long time. As far as he was concerned, there was no reason for leaving the English church.[6]

The other converts were even less fortunate than Newman. Shortly after Newman's conversion Pusey published another "letter" in the *Churchman*. This time the subject was Frederick Oakeley's pending move. Pusey urged that "no contradictions at home" should lead anyone to abandon his duty to the religion in which he was baptised. The English church had all the sacraments that were available in the Roman church, if only potential converts could believe as Pusey believed. The cure for the Romeward tendency was confession, and Pusey spelled out explicit instructions on how Oakeley should make his confession. All of this was printed in the *English Churchman;* and thus the idea that there was something morally wrong with the converts was begun. Every issue of the *Churchman* contained some form of attack on the morals of those who had gone over. There is nothing in any of these attacks that cannot be found in Keble's final works. God had called English Christians to the Church of England, and nothing short of the miraculous should cause a man to abandon his duty to that church.[7]

In Keble's works and correspondence of 1845 through the end of his life, we find a kind of religion that is almost impossible to describe in detail except for its anti-Romanism. As far as can be told, Keble sincerely believed that the Church of England, or at least part of it, was Catholic, but in his efforts to promote that kind of Catholicism, we find Keble, and much more so Pusey, working mainly by assertion. The church was Catholic because they believed and said it was Catholic. Such an argument is not wholly

[6]John Griffin, *The Oxford Movement: A Revision* (Edinburgh: Pentland Press, 1984) 80-81.

[7]Ibid., 82.

persuasive, but it was well-suited to the occasion if we remember the reputation of both men in the Church of England. In his "Preface" of 1847 Keble enlarged on what might be called a "religion of the heart." The English church was the loving mother to all her dutiful children, and even if she were not, no child should complain about the circumstances in which he had been born and raised. Those who went to Rome would be forced to look upon those whom they had left behind as simply ignorant pagans, which was impossible since the English church, as every Anglican knew, abounded in saints. Of special importance was the example set by George Herbert and William Ken. They had lived through perilous times in the church and had witnessed for the holiness of the church by their sufferings.[8]

The English church might endure some embarrassments at the hand of the Privy Council, but because it was truly Catholic, it would never "formally admit" heresy into its teachings.[9] Bishops like Renn Hampden and judicial decisions like the Gorham and Denison verdicts were trials to a man's moral character, not his faith, because the church had always had its share of imperfections.

The most powerful expression of the Anglo-Catholic position was made in 1865 by Dr. Pusey in his book *The Church of England: A Portion of Christ's One, Holy Catholic Church, and a Means of Restoring Visible Unity. An Eirenicon, in a Letter to the Author of 'The Christian Year.'* Almost everyone who has studied the work has taken his interpretation from the word *eirenicon* in the title, but the ecumenical or "peace-making elements" in the book, so far as they may be said to exist at all, are clearly of secondary importance to Pusey's defense of the Catholic claims of the English church. This Pusey did primarily by flat assertion. Even a reviewer for one of the Anglo-Catholic journals noted that Pus-

---

[8]Thus Keble wrote of Bishop Ken, "Though in a manner cast out of the Church of his baptism, would not wander from it, but abode by its door." "Endurance of Church Imperfections," in *Sermons, Occasional and Academical,* 2nd ed. (Oxford: James Parker, 1847) 320.

[9]Keble to Lady Blough, 28 August 1850, Miscellaneous Collection, Keble College, Oxford.

ey's arguments were perhaps too subjective in nature to be of sufficient use in his arguments against Manning's recent pamphlets.[10]

The most effective part of the eirenicon was in the hundred odd pages on Marian devotions and dogmas in the Church of Rome. Whatever might be the problems in the Church of England, the Roman church taught or at least allowed practices, writings, and beliefs that gave every appearance of idolatry. Without subtracting from Pusey's genius and industry in constructing such an argument, it must be said that the ideas in the anti-Roman offensive were in large measure Keble's and, through Keble, taken into the polemic that was a regular feature in the Anglican press. The result of Pusey's volume, Keble's ministry and writings, and the more vigorous assertions of the Anglo-Catholic press was to balance the various difficulties as presented by the bishops or the Privy Council against the hard-core idolatry of the Roman system. Catholics sometimes made their condition worse by taking on extraordinary devotions to the Blessed Virgin or conducting novenas to the Virgin for Pusey's conversion; and Newman's moderation on the subject of the devotions and dogmas that surrounded the *Theotokos* was ignored.

Keble is the most valuable witness for the interpretation of the eirenicon that I am proposing, for he knew that it would not be well-received by Roman Catholics and wrote to his brother Tom as to its likely effect.

> ... if I don't mistake Pusey will soon have enough to do to brush away the flies + wasps in which he has plunged himself by writing his last book. It is meant in all with kindness, + will I expect prove an eirenicon in the end. But for the moment it will affront them greviously.[11]

Yet Keble, a few months later, faulted Newman for his "complaining" attitude towards Pusey's work.

---

[10]"Dr. Pusey's *Eirenicon*," *Union Review* 4 (Winter 1866): 11: "It may be that Dr. Pusey lays too great a stress on the subjective consciousness of possessing the grace of the Sacrament, as a proof that it is really there."

[11]John Keble to Thomas Keble, September 1865, Williams Collection, Lambeth Palace Library, London.

(1) he seemed to me to take a very unpleasing view of the book, wondering how it could call itself an *eirenicon,* and almost out of temper with it: and (2) it disappointed me after I had been led by your letter to hope that moderate R.C.'s would take it as it is meant and sympathize with it. . . . And altogether his sayings in this very letter seem to me to confirm yours, to the effect that while born R.C.'s are not to be held committed to these extreme ideas, it will be a hard fight for any convert who wishes to keep clear of them.[12]

Parts of this letter are a distinct echo of what Keble had been warning prospective converts of since at least 1847. The converts would be asked to approve all of the Roman devotions to the Blessed Virgin and the other saints, and according to at least one of the converts (Frederic Oakeley), the argument was highly effective.[13] Keble would never allow the validity of Newman's argument that devotions were "free" and not required in the Roman church. Yet there was a small inconsistency in Keble's argument, for one of the positive aspects of his Anglicanism was the example provided by those of conspicuous holiness in the English church. The convert would also be asked to deny that such holiness existed in those whom he knew to be "models of Christian goodness."

Think of bringing one's self to regard those very persons as no more than very good heathens and their works as no portion nor fruit of the Unspeakable Gift![14]

Thus the "moral instinct" of most "English Churchmen of the Anglo-Catholic school" was clearly on the side of the English church; and it was no matter that such an instinct might operate in opposition to "seeming logical or historical evidence."[15]

---

[12]Quoted in Harry P, Liddon, *Life of the Rev. E. B. Pusey,* 4 vols. (London: Macmillan and Co., 1898) 4:124.

[13]Frederick Oakeley, *The Leading Topics of Dr. Pusey's Recent Work Reviewed in a Letter to the Most Rev. H. E. Manning* (London: Longman's, Green, & Co., 1866) 12.

[14]Keble, "Preface," *Sermons, Occasional and Academical,* xxx.

[15]Ibid., xvii.

As for the divisions or imperfections in the English church, the Roman church had its own problems on that score. As he said in another letter to Pusey on the subject of his eirenicon and Newman's failure to understand its purpose,

> How strange it is that he should entirely forget your having written entirely on the defensive: as though you had been challenging H.E.M. [Manning] and not replying to his challenge. But one can see that he is not altogether easy in his position. And all the world can see that at any rate Rome has now no special right to twit us with our unhappy divisions.[16]

The above is a fair summary of Keble's apologetic for himself and for the English church. Every religion had its problems, and certitude of faith was an impossibility. As he told William Copeland, "As to being free from intellectual perplexities, I have long ago ceased to hope for any such thing in this world."[17] A good Anglican should "cheerfully" abandon any such hopes for himself and concentrate rather on the practical duties of his religion.[18]

Keble died in March of the following year, and shortly after his burial, plans were made for some kind of tribute to him. The idea of founding a college indicated the great importance and influence of Keble on the Church of England. One of Pusey's biographers described Keble's influence as greater "than any other man of his generation," greater even than that of Dr. Pusey himself. The biographer urged that Keble's influence exerted itself in two different directions—towards "complete submission to the See of Rome" or "steadfast . . . allegiance to the Anglican Communion."[19]

Newman argued that Keble's principles led to Rome, though no one could have known that in 1833. Pusey took the opposite side. The teachings of John Keble led to a deeper appreciation of

---

[16]Liddon, *Life of the Rev. E. B. Pusey,* 4:130.

[17]Keble to William Copeland, Lent, 1846, Keble Letters, Department 9, Lambeth Palace Library, London.

[18]Keble, "Endurance of Imperfections," *Sermons, Occasional and Academical,* 307.

[19]Liddon, *Life of the Rev. E. B. Pusey,* 4:140.

the Catholic heritage of Anglicanism. Perhaps the word *steadfast* is too strong to describe Keble's unique position in the church, but there can be no question as to where Keble's primary loyalties rested. On both sides, however, there is at least one level of agreement: Keble was far more influential than even his most devoted readers ever knew.

Selected Bibliography

Manuscript Collections

Letters of John Keble to John Taylor Coleridge. Four vols. Coleridge Collection. Bodleian Library, Oxford.

Letters of John Keble to E. B. Pusey. Three vols. Pusey House, Oxford.

Letters of John Keble and Others. Keble Collection. Keble College, Oxford.

Letters of John Keble to John Henry Newman. Three vols. Oratory of St. Philip. Birmingham, England.

Keble Family Letters. Williams Collection. Lambeth Palace Library, London.

Letters and Correspondence of Isaac Williams. Lambeth Palace Library, London.

Keble Miscellany. Keble Collection. Bodleian Library, Oxford.

Books

Battiscombe, Georgina. *John Keble: A Study in Limitations*. New York: Alfred A. Knopf, 1964.

Beek, Wilhelm. *John Keble's Literary and Religious Contribution to the Oxford Movement.* Nijmegen: Academic Centrale, 1959.

Church, Richard. *The Oxford Movement, 1833-1845: A Personal Memoir.* London: Macmillan and Co., 1891.

Coleridge, John T. *A Memoir of the Rev. John Keble.* Fifth ed., Oxford: James Parker, 1880.

Griffin, John. "Newman and Others [Keble]." In *Newman: A Bibliography of Secondary Studies.* Alexandria VA: Christendom Press, 1980.

_____. *The Oxford Movement: A Revision.* Edinburgh: Pentland Press, 1984.

Ingram, Kenneth. *John Keble.* London: Philip Allan, 1933.

Keble, John. *The Christian Year.* London: Bickers and Son, 1875.

_____. *Lectures on Poetry.* Translated and edited by Edwin K. Francis. Two vols. Oxford: James Parker, 1912.

_____. *Lyra Innocentium.* London: James Parker, 1902.

_____. *Occasional Papers and Reviews.* Edited by Harry P. Liddon. Oxford: James Parker, 1895.

_____. *Sermons, Academical and Occasional.* Second ed. Oxford: James Parker, 1848.

_____. *Sermons, Occasional and Parochial.* Oxford: James Parker, 1868.

_____. *The State in Its Relation with the Church.* Edited by Harry P. Liddon. Oxford: James Parker, 1869.

_____. *Village Sermons on the Baptismal Service.* Oxford: James Parker, 1869.

Liddon, Harry P. *Life of the Rev. E. B. Pusey.* Four vols. London: Macmillan's and Co., 1898.

Lock, Walter. *John Keble: A Biography.* London: Methuen, 1893.

Martin, Brian. *John Keble: Priest, Professor and Poet.* London: Croom Helm, 1976.

Mozley, Thomas. *Reminiscences, Chiefly of Oriel College and the Oxford Movement.* Two vols. Boston: Houghton Mifflin Co., 1882.

Newman, John Henry. *Apologia Pro Vita Sua.* Edited by Wilfred Ward. London: Everyman Books, 1913.

_____. *Correspondence with John Keble and Others, 1839-1845*. Edited by the Fathers at the Birmingham Oratory. London: Longman's, Green, & Co., 1917.

_____. *Difficulties Felt by Anglicans*. Two vols. Westminster MD: Christian Classics, 1968.

_____. "John Keble." In *Essays, Critical and Historical*. 10th ed. London: Longman's, Green, & Co., 1880.

_____. *Letters and Correspondence*. Edited by Anne Mozley. Two vols. London: Longman's, Green, and Co., 1891.

_____. *Letters and Diaries of John Henry Newman*. Edited by Charles S. Dessain, Thomas Gornall, and Gerald Tracey, S. J. Oxford: Clarendon Press, 1961– .

Newsome, David. *The Wilberforces and Henry Manning: The Parting of Friends*. Cambridge MA: Harvard University Press, 1966.

Articles

Chadwick, Owen. "The Limitations of Keble." *Theology* 67 (Spring 1964): 46-52.

Griffin, John. "The Anglican Response to Newman's Conversion." *Faith and Reason* 3 (Spring 1977): 17-34.

_____. "John Keble and the *Quarterly Review*." *Review of English Studies* 29 (November 1978): 452-56.

_____. "John Keble: Radical." *Anglican Theological Review* 43 (June 1971): 167-73.

_____. "John Keble: A Report from the Devil's Advocate." *Historical Magazine of the Protestant Episcopal Church* 48 (June 1979): 219-34.

_____. "The Meaning of 'National Apostasy': A Note on Newman's *Apologia*." *Faith and Reason* 2 (Spring 1976): 19-33.

McGreevy, Michael. "John Keble on the Anglican Church and the Church Catholic." *Heythrop Journal* 5 (Spring 1964): 18-28.

_____. "John Keble's Way to Christian Unity." *One in Christ* 1 (Spring 1965): 53-61.

Martin, Brian A. "Wordsworth, Faber and Keble: Commentary on a Triangular Relationship." *Review of English Studies* 26 (November 1975): 436-42.

Index